THE
BOMB
THAT
BLEW
UP
GOD

AND
OTHER SERIOUS POEMS
BY
FREDDY NIAGARA FONSECA

The Bomb That Blew Up God

Freddy Niagara Fonseca

Copyright © 2020 Freddy Niagara Fonseca

Published by 1st World Publishing
P.O. Box 2211, Fairfield, Iowa 52556
tel: 641-209-5000 • fax: 866-440-5234
web: www.1stworldpublishing.com

First Edition

Library of Congress Control Number: 2020936464
ISBN: 978-1-4218-3655-3

I dedicate this book to my earliest mentor and critic, Joe Palmieri, actor, who introduced me to American poetry. Some people think that I'm a born poet. Sorry to disappoint you, but when I was younger I didn't care for poetry. Not in South America where I was born and grew up. And not in the Netherlands where I tried to grow up some more. I started liking poetry long after high school. But the real fireworks came when I was living in Rome, Italy. One day I went on a leisurely stroll through the gorgeous Villa Borghese Gardens with my friend Joe Palmieri. We stopped at a statue of Lord Byron sitting on one of Rome's seven hills overlooking the city to read a short verse on the pedestal from his *"Childe Harold"*

> *But I have lived, and have not lived in vain:*
> *My mind may lose its force, my blood its fire,*
> *And my frame perish even in conquering pain,*
> *But there is that within me which shall tire*
> *Torture and Time, and breathe when I expire.*

and lightning struck: BOOM! I started writing poems the next day. I showed some to Joe who immediately encouraged me to get myself acquainted with American poetry. I committed to reading, reading, reading like a starved 'poemeater' (a species that reads poems to survive) day after day, for many years. I've probably read at least 20,000 poems in five languages. I continued traveling in Europe, and ultimately landed in the US in 1986 to immerse myself further into American lore, culture and poetry.

> *And now we have this book.*
> *Thank you on the other side, Joe.*
> *I wish I could hand you a copy now.*

I'm grateful for a great many friends who over the years have advised, guided and inspired me (unbeknownst to some at times) through this magical garden called poetry. Several names come to mind: Diana Quinlan-Rugh, Charlie Hopkins, Glenda S. Pliler, Rex Kutzli, Christine Fonseca, Michael Johnson, Raven Garland, Tony Ellis, Catherine Castle, Job Conger, Rolf Erickson, Stuart Libby, John Edgette, Angela Mailander, Ken Chawkin, Gretchen Langstaff Schaffer, Nathan Zumstein, George Attwood, Jordy Yager, Burton Milward and the incomparable Bill Godfrey.

Thank you all "mucho" much!

Jacket design and book layout
Freddy Niagara Fonseca

Please visit my blog
fonseca-poems.org

WHAT PEOPLE SAY

From haiku to narrative free verse, his exploration of form, rhyme and rhythm is almost a compedium of modern poetic style. The tone is varied too - from playful humor to earnest poignancy - but the poems are artfully arranged to lead the reader smoothly from one emotion to next. And then there is the breadth of subject matter, which allows the reader a close-up view of the vastness of human experience, across the globe and deep within, through the poet's eyes. Freddy's poems are accessible on the surface, easy to read, yet layered with deeper meaning for those willing to spend more time with them.

—Monica Hadley, entrepreneur and host of the podcast *Writers' Voices with Monica and Caroline*

Drawing from a wide cultural background, Freddy Niagara Fonseca, skips, dances and delights his way through this wonderful collection of poems.

—Tony Ellis, author of *There is Wisdom in Walnuts*

I loved this vast, complex, yet simple book of wonderful poetry. I recommend this book of sublime intensity to any true reader.

—Rudy Wilson, National Award Winning Author of several novels

Here is a highly educated mind, taking from a thorough familiarity with the forms of poetry only what fits most fluidly to his purpose.

—Karla Christensen, poet, muralist, illustrator, Ecuador

This collection of works is distinctive — certainly original and eclectic, deeply sobering and uniquely stylized.

—Rodney Charles, author of the bestselling *Every Day A Miracle Happens*

What a variety of emotions in these poems! Some whimsical and calling to be read aloud, some elegantly musical with a touch of Shakespeare.

—Jeffrey Moses, Author of *Oneness: Great Principles Shared by All Religions*

This impressive volume is one that we can pick up at bedtime and open any page for mind travel. We are reminded that we are part of the world of nature.

—Gretchen Langstaff Schaffer, dancer, BA Fine Arts in Dance The Juilliard School

From the seductions of dance to the secrets of creation, Fonseca has prepared a banquet of verse ... a transcendent explosion of creative joy and wry humor.

—Debra Smith, Educational Kinesiologist, Watercolorist, Potter, Poet

What can I say about these stunning poems? The poet himself came to my rescue: On page 109 I found: *After Reading an Obscure Volume of Unusual Poetry* which describes Fonseca's own poetry perfectly.

—Angela Mailander, Professor Emerita of Comparative Literature, Jiangsu University of Science and Technology, P.R. China

Colors explode, surprises abound, twists and turns and excursions into seemingly unrelated (to me) areas that all seem to end up in a magnificent whole that in the end leaves me in a fascinating space.

—Brad Moses, singer songwriter, recording artist, arranger

Comments on *Books*: It captures the spiritual dimension of reading and writing, and the connection to eternity that we make through books. I've often had the same feelings — the multitude of books overwhelms me with awareness of my mortality and yet at the same time connects me to something immortal. Nice job.

—Jendi Reiter, editor of WinningWriters.com and author of *Bullies in Love* and *Two Natures*

The Bomb That Blew Up God is at times whimsical, sobering, always illuminating.

—*The Culture Buzz*, John Busbee, founder and producer

He lives outside of the comfortable boundaries we are accustomed to but his poetry brings things back from wherever he is. I would say, 'Just open the book.'

—Ron Ringsrud, Author of *Emeralds: A Passionate Guide*

I could not stop. When each poem ended, I was compelled to read the next. Each poem touched me with a recognition of something strong within myself, joy, fear, surety, joy again.

—Michael Borden, architect, author of *Vastu Architecture*, New Zealand

Like music and dance, the poems sing and express a rhythm connecting them to all the arts. There is balance and charm, rhythm and harmony, everything needed to create an entertaining and enlightened read.

—John Schirmer...... forty years a print maker, painter, and sculptor

I'm amazed by the power and gripping beauty of his prayer like poetry. How could a mere mortal be so descriptive, the senses so real?

—James Dean Claitor, former film producer and freelance writer

Comments on *Olé, Bolero*: Great poem, such gusto and wonderful play, celebrating the sexuality and sensuality of the language that conveys it. All those great names and Spanish words. Bravo.

—Craig Deininger, PhD, Assistant Professor of Creative Writing, MIU, *Leaves from the World Tree*: Selected Poems of Craig Deininger and Dennis Patrick Slattery.

His poem "*Antarctica*" begins with an exploration of geographical extremes, from the ice and cold of Antarctica to the greenness and warmth of Trinidad. But as we move deeper into his poem, we notice that terrestrial geography becomes a metaphor for exploring his geography of the soul.

—James L. Shead, technical writer, ret., Certified Divine Mother Healer

Acknowledgements

"Dark Velvet" *The Neovictorian/Cochlea*, 2004. "Antarctica" *Pivot*, 2004, *Winning Writers*, 2004. "Kaleidoscope" *The Neovictorian/ Cochlea*, 2004, *The Iowa Source*, 2005. "Seeing a Map of Greece Across the Sky" *The Eclectic Muse*, 2004. "Out of Darker Grace" *The Dryland Fish*, 2003. "Carnival in Rio" *This Enduring Gift*, 2010. "Poetry Dances, Olé" *This Enduring Gift*, 2010. "Fire Dance — An Invocation of the Light" *This Enduring Gift*, 2010. "Statue of an Enraged Lion" *The Eclectic Muse*, 2004, *This Enduring Gift*, 2010. "Realms of Stone" *The Neovictorian/Cochlea*, 2006. "These Three Words" *Passive Fists - An Anthology by Poets for Peace*, 2004. "A Dove in Times of War" Passive Fists - An Anthology by Poets for Peace, 2004. "Bridge Under Construction" *The Eclectic Muse*, 2004. "Spring Pick Up" *The Fairfield Weekly Reader*, 2019. "A Zebra Moment" *Inquiring Mind*, 2006. "On a Medieval Painting of the Fall of Man" *This Enduring Gift*, 2010. "Falling Down a Manhole" *Art Scene*, 2005. "After a Swim" *The Dryland Fish*, 2003. "The Chimes of the Clock at the Courthouse" *The Fairfield Ledger*, 2004. "The New York City Zoo" *This Enduring Gift*, 2010. "Your Face" *The Eclectic Muse*, 2004. "Books" *The Neovictorian/ Cochlea*, 2006, *Winning Writers*, 2006, *This Enduring Gift*, 2010. "Eternal Source" *Pivot*, 2004, *The Neovictorian/Cochlea*, 2005. "Awestruck at Niagara Falls" *This Enduring Gift*, 2010. "The Doe" *This Enduring Gift*, 2010. "Spring Is Like a Young, Wonderful Woman" *The Eclectic Muse*, 2003 as "Spring, the Goddess". "The Quiet Way of Unforgotten Trees" *Tower Poetry Society*, 2003. "Giant Sequoia" *This Enduring Gift*, 2010. "The Language of the Trees" *This Enduring Gift*, 2010, *Sierra Club Southeast Iowa, the Leopold Group*, Spring 2011. "Distant Mountains" *Candelabrum Poetry Magazine*, 2005. "White Blossoms" *Candelabrum Poetry Magazine*, 2004. "Tango in Buenos Aires" *Telephone Booth Iowa*, 2020.

Other books by Freddy Niagara Fonseca

This Enduring Gift - A Flowering of Fairfield Poetry with a Foreword by Donovan

CONTENTS

SHARDS OF LIGHT

DARK VELVET

We are all in the gutter,
but some of us are looking at stars.
—Oscar Wilde

I

Some memories shine like living precious stones
Now scattered on the dark velvet here before me:
    Rubies, red with liquid passion;
    Opals, playful, transparent, pure;
    One rose quartz, heart-shaped and glowing;
    Sapphires, azure like some pensive gaze;
    Diamonds, strangely lucid and serene,
Emerging briefly from
A universe now lost,
Or hidden...

II

Such are the gems I remember from myth long ago,
Before being scattered across the dark firmament:
    Glimmering now like distant fires;
    Sparkling in the vastnesses of space;
    Beaming from the farthest galaxies;
    Quietly gazing down through time;
    Slowly orbiting inside my brain,
And steadily gleaming like on
Deep dark velvet—
Remote, alive...

ANTARCTICA

I

Cold! Cold! Totally cold! Colder than Alaska or Siberia;
Colder than the North Pole; cold like a frozen soul
You are, oh age-old Antarctica.

Measureless and empty plains with silences as white and deep as
    death
Descended on me there, and frost besieged the air
From rocks of ice around Antarctica.

Dark and shapeless were the nights while somewhere deep in
    space, the Milky Way
Rose beaming like the dawn, but never would the sun,
And I withdrew behind Antarctica.

II

Warm...warm...lovely warm...warmer than the Congo, Spain or
    India...
Warmer than a bonfire has been my old desire
For always green, tropical Trinidad.

Riverbanks and stars arise, despite the walls of ice I once evoked
Around Antarctica as I am reaching for
My always green, tropical Trinidad.

Oh, there's the warmth of old in newfound Trinidad.
Royal are the palm trees, timeless in the evening breeze
In always green, tropical Trinidad.

III

Long ago there was a time my heart was helpless in Antarctica
With blizzards all about, where life was but a shout
Across a desolate Antarctica.

Dim is the light on snowy nights when I remember old Antarctica.
The cold is in my past because I changed at last,
And so did you, oh old Antarctica.

Warm is the light on starry nights, shining on my Trinidad.
The warmth within her lovely name has now become a joyful flame
Around my soul, my age-old Trinidad.

The Stone Age and the Internet

When cavemen discovered fire
by rubbing two sharp rocks
against each other, they had no
concept yet of complexities
like the Internet ages ahead.

These days computers will strike
quick sparks between people
aiming at a better life,
kindling many a lonely heart seeking
purpose now and maybe love.

Cave fires sizzled, and as people
warmed their hands before them,
they fancied savage flames
inside their caves in stead of
fleeting texts or distant lovers.

Romance was quite different back then;
more direct I'm sure and hot like hell.
But even though courting may seem
cautious nowadays, that first spark still
envisions light, warmth, love and home.

KALEIDOSCOPE

We have all nursed illusions:
give us the right ones.
And all of us dream Dreams:
let us dream bright ones.
—Joe Ruggier

I'm a man of many shards
and, unless seen together in
all of its fractured wonder,
as incomplete as any.

One flick of the hand—I
turn into something new al-
together, leaving what's
old and gone changed for good.

Numerous facets shift and still
resist fully falling into place,
except for this flaky, shattered
jumble of lights reaching out.

My fragmentation negates
the way I used to be, and there's
an unseen rift I cannot touch
behind these splinters of deceit.

And yet my flickering purples,
yellows, and other clueless
colors impulsively glimmer every
time like stars, scattered and all.

Held against the sun or nearby
lamp, I quickly tend to appear
what I must have been before:
poised, light, and all in one piece.

BLACK HOLE

I used to go through life quite flat-footed. Back
then, the sidewalk would stick to my heels,
but I've grown up quite a bit, touching the stars
way up here. Far below there's Earth, still kicking.
My body? It's being nebulous and probably
stretching all over the Milky Way right now.

My heart is somewhere in the middle, and it's
awfully wide. In fact, there's a huge gap in my
chest and I'm breathing the Universe in and out
night and day. A black hole is all that I really am,
and I've dropped all contact with matter for sure,
but hey, I'm enjoying my space here immensely.

Arriving at Twin Peaks
for an Exceptionally Bright Night View
on San Francisco

What a sea of lights all across town tonight,
overwhelming me with more than awe.
What a sea of stars all over that dark, yet
uncannily bright night sky—more than I ever
saw! It seems the City unwittingly mirrors
the night as much with lights below as above.
The stars just take your breath away, but so
does all of this blazing vista on San Francisco.
There, the sea so scintillating in the Bay —
the City, intensely glistening far and wide —
this brisk breeze blowing through my body —
this twin presence of celestial *and* terrestrial
light . . . It's all-overpowering, almost too much.
These days, the more I get to think of how many
ambiguities still are lurking inside me that I
don't yet dare to face, the more something
seems to want me at some far—off plateau of
total light I'm yet to see some unknown time.
Not that I need to give up the rapture of these
glorious moments on arriving at the peak of
this breathless experience. I'm being pulled into
it head to toe, and almost wanting the world to
forever STOP at this dazzling view fantastically
vibrating through the night. It pulsates
with myriad glimmerings of *so much life*,
pouring out of that double blaze of nocturnal
LIGHT unifying *ALL* . . . And all night long
an immense *something* brightly engulfs the
Bay, the City, the Peaks . . . *unutterably* grand
and darkly haunting . . . Strange . . . this vast,
oceanic wind washing headlong over me —
I could step into it . . . NOW . . .

SALIVATING OVER A STILL LIFE BY FRENCH PAINTER PIERRE BONNARD

Those peaches, plums, apples and grapes,
peeking at me from that pink fruit bowl,
are seriously trying to lure me into
this cheerful painting at the museum.

The background's myriad patches of color
quickstep all over the canvas, not unlike
those on Pierre Bonnàrd's busy palette
which I've been trying to fathom for years.

To conjure up all of this fullness and light,
he must've mixed his pigments like a wizard.
There's a world of succulent, pictorial
art there for the gourmet in all of us:

Bonnard's teasing tints and shades just
prance around this lush cornucopia of life,
and all from scratch. How deft his brush was.
Some call this Post-Impressionism.

I'd call it something far less artsy.
As this not so still, French still life stirs my
salivating glands, magic spells from orchards
splash over my color-drunk eyes like crazy.

Ah, all you merry taste bud teasers — you
and Bonnard are so good at whetting my
appetite, enticing me time and again to
reach out for one glorious, impossible bite.

Seeing a Map of Greece Across the Sky

A map across the sky appears: the calm Aegean waters meet
Olympian mountains where the coastline always sees
an endless boundlessness.

I'm watching blobby shapes of puffy, changing clouds
forming contours shaping islands by the coast of Greece,
dappled on the blue today.

I climbed a Grecian hilltop on another day and found a valley
holding pillars, woods of silence by a godlike bay in Greece,
sloping to an azure sea.

That's when I knew antiquity. The light was one bright beam
across a stage where curtains had been raised, and Greece
was gazing at immortal waves.

I fell in love with Greece, yet had to leave that day, but now
she's
coming back like mountains rise before one's view in Greece,
and there's her golden smile again.

Oh, Helen of Troy — Poseidon — your oracles — Delphi — Zeus!
Oh, for your mystery — Athens! To you, oh sacred, ancient Greece
I shall return and hail your shrines.

See how the sea approaching Greece appears across the sky,
and how, like in the olden times, Mankind marvels still at
all the grandeur that was Greece.

OUT OF DARKER GRACE

When the Universe withdraws
inside the Dark, and
nothing else remains in space,
the stars across the sky
resume their ever-loving,
never-ending wake.

They've reached around the globe
since Time onetime
began its lonely, outward leap,
and held, with matchless care,
the quiet,
unborn realms of night.

Darkness may have been a cause
until this round, but now that
Time's unveiling who we are,
a secret force delivers
worlds from
once a darker place.

Cognizant of life evolving
from within itself,
a light appears
behind the veil, despite
whatever gloom had
ruled before.

Remnants of eons, far,
are strewn across the sky
where newer stars attain
possession of the space
between what's yet to come
and prior darker grace.

Starry nights perhaps
have known this all along,
for all upon the universal map,
they manifest
and dot a radiant firmament
with budding lights.

Wisdom must have been
their share and warmth at heart,
and perhaps their only wish
is being of such service here
as Time goes by on Earth
to bring the Dawn.

DARK NIGHT OF A SOUL

I

Night,
oh starry Night,
with your stars so bright, arching over me on high.
Although you are dark, a secret light pervades the sky,
a light brighter than day.

II

Night,
oh glorious Night,
with your deep wisdom whispering out of your space,
fondly breathing cooling breezes to my upturned face—
you take my darkest thoughts away.

III

Night,
majestic Night,
I've lived with your light to cross the abyss, the horrid dark.
Oh take me into your light. Ignite this darkest of sparks.
Let me dwell in your light.

IV

Night,
oh tender Night,
how pure is your light unfolding aloft.
Your infinite presence is soothing and soft.
Oh Night, I'm safe inside your light.

V

Night,
oh starry Night,
with your stars so bright, arching over me on high.
Although you are dark, a secret light pervades the sky,
God's light . . . God's . . . God . . .

THE SUN AND I

I'm lying in the sun,
part of me that is.
It reaches my face
through my small window.

Every now and then
I shift a bit to keep
aligned with its warmth
as time moves on.

Science says the earth turns;
the sun doesn't move,
but of course they're wrong.
The sun moves and so do I.

An Alpine Panorama

The Creator's Dream

I

Massive, snowcapped, inaccessible and alone,
The mountain stands, watching the night.
No man will tread this region now,
For towering darkness sits on every ridge and peak.
>   Ages unfold—
>   Eras go by
For eons on end. The mountain rests.

II

Flanked by granite chasms, and giant ice walls,
The summit rushes to the stars!
No barriers to audacity
Confront this bold intent, and nothing seems too high.
>   Heaven beckons—
>   Heaven waits.
Only of heaven the mountain dreams.

III

Slowly looming, coming from some different world,
The sun ascends the morning sky.
Grandly the night retreats, and soon
Its shadows follow, fading where the light is born.
>   Dawn has risen—
>   Dawn is here,
Banning the dark from the mountain range.

IV

Flooded with all the glow a rising sun can bring,
The mountain hails the day.
No man will tread this region now,
For blinding brilliance climbs on every ridge and peak.
> Eons come—
> Eons pass.
A blazing beacon, the mountain beams.

V

Teeming clouds assemble over its lower crests,
And blizzards lash their flanks with snow.
Lower still, far below the snow line,
The world lies safe in valleys, lakes and endless plains.
> Rivers flow—
> Rivers glisten
Close to the mountain's heart.

VI

Hanging glaciers cover much of the mountain's face
With streams of broad and frozen tears.
Gigantic blocks of ice break off,
And suddenly, a distant past comes thundering down!
> Earth trembles—
> Earth remembers.
Eras collapse. Eras form.

VII

Even though some cliffs around the timber line may
Try to pierce the sky, a dream of green resists
Inside the deeper stone . . .
Someday the rock will split, and earth—this humble earth—
> Will break the mold,
> Shake the cold
And rise with flora, fauna, Man.

VIII

Gravity has a way with matter, conquering all,
While those alive seek out the sky!
From horizon to horizon,
The far space of heaven arches over the world.
      Heaven beams—
      Heaven beckons.
Clouds disperse now while twilight descends.

IX

High in remote splendor, basking day and night,
Dwells a mountain, calm, sublime.
Serenely rapt in grand repose,
The top beholds the sky, the light, the air, the world.
      The world beckons—
      The world beams,
Created in a dream ages ago.

X

Covered with snow and thousands of colors and lights,
The mountain briefly stirs at dusk,
For Man may tread this region now,
Where matter, life and love unite to touch the heart.
      The heart exults—
      The heart soars
While the summit waits. The mountain beams . . .

DANCES, MUSIC, MAGIC

CARNIVAL IN RIO

Row after row of color, costumes, glitter galore—
Wave after wave of thundering feet and deafening voices—
Billow on billow of prancing, advancing masses of dancers—
    We're dancing the samba, the samba, the samba in
        Rio—Rio de Janeiro, Brazil.
We shake our shoulders, bottoms, and bellies to the beat...
    Of the bongos,
        the bongos,
            the bongos.

Hours and hours of dancing, singing, laughing and fun—
Day after day of cheer in the fiery heat of roasting Rio—
Night after night of feverish lust and great, fantastic vices—
    We know no worries whenever we dance in the streets of
        Rio—Rio de Janeiro, Brazil.
We twist and turn and stamp, and thus we succumb...
    To the rhythm,
        the rhythm,
            the rhythm.

Beat after beat of raging blood and rising desire—
Song after song of attraction and lure of the sexes—
Dance after dance of reveling, heaving oceans of bodies—
    We're dancing the samba, the samba, the samba in
        Rio—Rio de Janeiro, Brazil.
We gasp and groan like all our ancestors did...
    In the Congo,
        the Congo,
            the Congo.

Stream after stream of dark, irresistible rhythms—
Wave after wave of hot, tremendous, African forces—
Billow on billow of burning, baking, boiling catharsis—
     We're back in the Congo—the Congo—the Congo—and
          Not in Rio de Janeiro, Brazil.
We join our fathers and mothers to shake and mate to the beat...
     Deep in the womb
        of the rhythm,
          the rhythm,
            the rhythm.

ODE TO MUSIC

Come now with harps
to join the tenors here
and touch the strings!
The flute will sing
to all the instruments we love.
Listen, violins and violas mingle
with the choir.

Clang all the gongs,
and sound the organ now,
and beat the drums!
We all intone
to music of the centuries.
Hear the bells and cymbals
coming to the fore.

Play now those runs
to bring that winning tune,
and spread delight!
Nature sings in all of us,
and there's a thrilling song.
Give in to sweet melodiousness
within your soul.

Hear now how those birds
combine their warbling notes
with vivid rhythms.
Truly, *they* are singing
from a harmony we've lost.
Silver carols ring, and spring
awakens in a trill.

Oh, let's have flowers,
rustling leaves, and always,
always happiness.
The woodwinds speak of
summer gardens, or are we hearing
songs of distant nightingales,
evoked by soft bassoons?

A warm andante
is unfolding from a tranquil pond
one early morning.
The swans are mute . . .
Mysteriously they drift along
on streams of perfect, timeless and
eternal beauty.

The pearly triplets
of the grand piano
join the waterfall.
Murmuring sources
bring reflections back of old.
Do you remember how lotuses would
float on rivulets?

Lakes would form then
while an ocean lingered
in a single note.
A mountain song
would soar within a symphony,
and hidden valleys
struck a grander chord.

Towering heavens
opened up to us
in days gone by.
The world was quiet
like a pause between two songs,
and we were far from here in love
upon a sunny hill.

A burning sun
resounds in baritones.
It is midday.
A simple ditty
sounds with children on a stroll.
A silence falls, and now a woman hums
behind a house.

The clarinet
resumes a previous theme,
and evening comes.
Guitars are heard!
They bring the gentle heartbeat
to the music we adored. The sun has set.
The moon is out.

Come now with brass!
A trumpet, and a voice
will lead the dance.
Hear the saxophones
with sharps, and flats, and quivering lilts!
The clock strikes twelve, but they won't stop
until the stars wane.

Contraltos rise
announcing dawn.
The boy sopranos
join with ever rising scales
and strike such crystal tones
that move even the angels. Hear their voices
climb into the skies!

We hear a prelude
to a realm of music
all but endless—
God Himself descends!
Let's sing and love and dance.
Ages bend above you. Sing that song.
Toll the bell.

A solo for the bass
transforms into a hymn.
The lead soprano sings
a haunting, final melody,
transcending understanding here on earth:
Oh Heavenly Father, now forevermore,
welcome me, Thy Newborn Child!

Music! You're truly ringing
from the harmonies
of love, sublime and pure.
Oh, song of songs.
No one can withstand such love.
The chorus sets with liquid gold. It's time.
Come, we must go home . . .

TANGO IN BUENOS AIRES

A touch of Argentina. Ahhh . . .
Sweeping dresses, blinking eyes,
Supple, rhythmical steps,
And *quite* unexpected turns!
A lot of space . . .
        And *there's* the tango
        On a hot, tropical night
        In a sultry ballroom
        In steamy . . .
Buenos Aires!

The blood is even hotter, uh!
Deftly the dancers glide on a
Saucy, rhythmical tune,
Glancing at one another
Again and again
        While humming *tangos*
        On hot, tropical nights,
        Where the moon sees
        Everything
        In steamy . . .
Buenos Aires!

Some of the lovers even sneak
Into the gardens *before* a
Tango is over! The rhythm
Goes on . . . , yet the moon will
Keep silent. Ahhh, but *that's*
        How *tangos* are danced
        On hot, tropical nights
        In the shadowy gardens
        Of steamy,
        Saucy,
        Sultry . . .
Buenos Aires!

POETRY DANCES, OLÉ!

Discourse on virtue and they pass by in droves.
Whistle and dance the shimmy, and you've got an
audience.
                    —Diogenes

Poetry Dances, olé! She really does.
Literary she isn't. Dancing is her thing.
She's burst upon the Writers' scene like no one before.
All she needs to start a saucy Samba, or dainty Waltz
        is her knack for Rythm . . .
        She's lifting a leg and arching her back . . . *There!*
She's already creating a thrill on the Page.

        My Muse, Poetry has taken me to a party tonight,
insisting on tackling all of the latest Salsas and Tangos—
anything goes. No time for Grammar—
too much fun at the Dance!
        She *can* be quite formal when writing Sonnets
        and well-Versed in Ballads,
but nah, not tonight.

        She won't be a wallflower ever.
She Prances with pros. You give her a Subject,
or Theme . . . In less than a minute, she wiggles
her Syntax to share with the crowd
        what a Sentence with gusto,
        a Turn of a Phrase,
and a body to Shake can do.

        The Classics, Nonfiction, and Romance
are eager to meet her.
Their Chapters won't Jive like her Verses, but hey,
all they want is to revel in Rhythm and join her in Print.
        Audaciously sensual
        with pert innuendo,
she kicks up her heels. She never holds back.

Wouldn't she love to Break-Dance with
hot Punctuation, or Slow-Dance
a stern Saraband with old-fashioned Spelling?
You bet! Adapting to Style on a whim,
she'll dance a Can-Can
and totally live it, or quickly
up the ante to a Tap-Dancing frenzy.

Right now she's off to Dance the Jig
with some of the Bards and Homer.
I'm sure she'll share a Court Dance with Shakespeare,
or Dance with Dante, flaunting Rhymes with dynamite Feet.
Stepping slowly, or quickly,
or all debonair,
she's always the life of the party.

Hey you, Nouns and Adverbs, make room for this gal—
her Syllables Rock.
Becoming entranced and pairing with Fiction,
she Dances the Limbo, Scribbling Scripts with her toe.
All of her Blank Verses
have been rehearsing
Merengues with Humorous Poems and Odes to Nature.

Bumping back to back and belly to belly,
she's awesome at tempting Language, Slang,
and Diction with magical moves. Look how those guys
are going out of their way to ogle her Couplets
as all of her Stanzas
get wilder when Dancing
all those seductive Boleros she knows.

Her Poetic License Skips, Dances, delights.
She's lately been known to be teaching
Cakewalks late at after-parties, strutting for hours
with fearless Free Verses, Critics and Limericks.
She hopes you'll simply enjoy
whatever *you* may Read between her Lines, but
hers is the joy of playing with Words that are willing.

Showing off and slyly unveiling her Meaning,
she aptly engages all of her Fancy while
totally rapt in the Dance. She has oomph, oh yes,
and really kicks ass, olé!
     She's having a ball and all heads turn to look
     and bodies Twist, and everyone cheers
as she Waltzes away to be Read in my Book.

MY CREOLE BELLE

A Cakewalk

We're dressed to the nines to win the cake.
We prance like the whites and bow and shake
Because the Sunday cakewalk has begun,
And now we strut and stride about for fun.
    We strut, shuffle, stride for fluffy frostings.
        We step and trot and tap.
            We walk, wiggle, whoop for sugar toppings.
           We jiggle, laugh and clap.

We Go for the Cakes, the Gals, the Cakes:
Short Gals, Round Cakes, Saucy Gals, Spice Cakes,
    Fat Gals, Layer Cakes, Busty Gals, Enormous Cakes!
Mmmmm, ANY cake, and YOU, my fluffy Creole Belle.
    Yum, gobble, slurp, smooch, mmmm!
Deep in the south, there's lots of cake and pretty gals,
And there I eat my cake, and have my yummy Creole Belle.

    I flaunt my long red coat again,
My tall silk hat and bright lacquered cane.
I'm out to parade and flirt with the gals,
And soon I'll eat my cake, and kiss my Belle.
We shake for cakes and lead the gals.
    We twist and fly and hop.
        We jump for kicks with sexy gals.
        We stamp and never stop.

We Reel for the Gals, the Cakes, the Gals:
Cupcakes, Creamy Gals, Cheesecakes, Cheeky Gals,
    Hot Cakes, Succulent Gals, Towering Cakes, Fantastic
        Gals!
Mmmmm, ANY gal, and YOU, my fluffy Creole Belle.
    Yum, gobble, slurp, smooch, mmmm!
Deep in the south, there's lots of cake and pretty gals,
And there I eat my cake, and have my yummy Creole Belle.

My Belle is round and sweet like cake,
And *she* will do whatever it takes
To step with a prize like me on her arm,
And doesn't she love to keep me warm.
We high-step left for angel food
    And giggle, romp and yell.
        We high-kick right for devil's food
          And huddle with the gals.

I'll Win the Cake and Prance with Belle.
I'll Have my Cake and Leave with Belle.
Yes, the Cake and Yes, with Belle.
And Once I'm Home with Cake and All,
      I'll Eat, and Grunt, and Smooch, and Mmmm!
But not just ANY cake or gal; just YOU, my fluffy Creole Belle.
      Yum, gobble, slurp, smooch, mmmm!
Deep in the south, there's lots of cake and pretty gals,
And there I eat my cake, and have my yummy Creole Belle.

Billy Belly's Boston Big Brass Band

A Nostalgic Divertimento in Four Episodes for Narrator,
Brass Band, Chorus, and Merry Audience

This composition is meant to serve no other purpose than
to cheer us up and entertain.
It will benefit from being read with childlike glee,
oomph, and good rhythm.

First Episode: Childhood
—The Parade—

One Two. One Two.
Boom Boom. Tara Boom.
Cheeng Boom. Oompah Boom.
Here they Come. Here they Come.
Oompah-Pah. Oompah-Pah.
Tara Boom. Drums Drums.
Sunday Morning. Here they Come.

Hear the Merry Slide Trombones.
Hear the Screaming Saxophones
Marching Down the Boston Streets.
Feel the Rhythm In your Feet.
Hear the Tenors, Altos, Flutes.
Hear the Stamping of the Boots.
Boots Boots. Boots Boots.

Over-Shoulder Tubas Blare
Boldly Moving to the Square.
Cheeng Boom. Over There.
Hear the Rumbling Drums and Bugles,
Jingling Johnnies, Singing Brass.
Hear the Fifes and Ringing Cymbals:
All the Town is Full of Brass.

There they Are. There they Are.
Billy Belly's Boston Boys.
Billy Belly's BOSTON—
Billy Belly's BOSTON—
Billy Belly's—CHEENG BOOM.
Billy Belly's—OOMPAH BOOM,
Billy Boom Tara Boom.

Billy Belly's B R A S S !
Billy Belly's B R A S S ! !
Billy Belly's B O S T O N ! ! !
Billy Belly's B O S T O N ! ! ! !
B I L L Y . . . B E L L Y' S . . .
B O S T O N . . . B I G . . .
B R A S S . . . B A N D ! ! ! ! !

Cheeng Boom.
LOUDER than Loud.
Cheeng Boom.
CHEERS from the CROWD.
Cheeng Boom. Oompah Boom.

Hurray.
	Hurray.
		Hurray.

			Great.
				Great.
					Great.

Second Episode: Adolescence
—*In the Streets and Squares of Boston*—

Ta—ra—ra Boom—de—ay!
What is going on today?
We're out to see my favorite band in Boston.

Friendly sunlight has been beaming, gleaming everywhere,
Brightening every glistening bell and valve and piston;
Every shining surface all around the sunny square.

> Everyone is glad today.
> Everyone is here today.
> Ta—ra—ra, Ta—ra—ra Boom—de—ay!

Never, never leave us, Billy.
Oh, we'll step along with you forever
Any Sunday down the streets and squares of Boston.

Ta—ra—ra Boom—de—ay!
Billy's Band is great today.
Billy in his towering bearskin shako,
Silver buttons, sash and gold-striped pantaloons,
Emblems, buckle belt and bulging jacket
Starts parading with his bandsmen Sunday afternoon.

> All the flags are out today.
> All the world is great today
> Ta—ra—ra, Ta—ra—ra Boom—de—ay!

Never, never leave us, Billy.
Oh, we'll march along with you forever
Any Sunday down the streets and squares of Boston.

Ta—ra—ra Boom—de—ay!
Let us sing and dance today.
Bandstand chorus members sing of "Stars and Glory."
All of us embrace the grandeur of the themes.
Overtures and marches speak of untold, epic stories.
All become one nation, sharing lofty dreams.

> Let us celebrate today.
> Let us all unite today.
> Ta—ra—ra, Ta—ra—ra Boom—de—ay!

Never, never leave us, Billy.
Oh, we'll sing along with you forever
Any Sunday down the streets and squares of Boston.

Third Episode: Maturity
—The Picnic by the River—

A thousand people gather by the riverbank
To hear a concert of the Boston Band.
No one seems to mind that tubas play off-key,
For moms are handing napkins out and cups of tea,
And yummy snacks are quickly passed around
To pretty tunes and crashing oompah sounds.
        Tara Boom, Clash Boom!
        Tara Cheeng, Cheeng, Boom
        On a Sunday afternoon.
        Boom Bang Oompah Boom!

While the players hardly spare their lungs,
Enormous loads of crackers land on tongues.
We munch away and loaf around on grass
Enjoying loud refrains in F on brass.
The band is playing merry, well-known songs
To please the happy, ever-eating throng.
        Tara Boom, Clash Boom!
        Tara Cheeng, Cheeng, Boom
        On a Sunday afternoon.
        Boom Bang Oompah Boom!

As the afternoon progresses, all agree that all those starches
Blend extremely well with feeling great and Sousa's marches.
Everyone is glad and most relaxed,
Looking for the goodies coming next.
See the countless faces glow.
See how all enjoy the show.
        Tara Boom, Clash Boom!
        Tara Cheeng, Cheeng, Boom
        On a Sunday afternoon.
        Boom Bang Oompah Boom!

While we feast on popcorn, creamy pies, and more,
Drums and trumpets step with cymbals to the fore.
We nibble, chatter, frisk about and hum,
And meet some far too long forgotten chums.

What a Sunday, what a picnic.
Nothing pesky, nothing hectic.
       Tara Boom, Clash Boom!
       Tara Cheeng, Cheeng, Boom
       On a Sunday afternoon.
       Boom Bang Oompah Boom!

It's getting late and Billy cannot play forever.
It's time now for the "Stars and Stripes Forever."
Tonight the band returns for dance and serenade,
And afterwards we'll join them for the night parade.
The picnic was a perfect treat
And Sousa's music quite a feast.
       Tara Boom, Clash . . .
       Tara Cheeng, Cheeng . . .
       Tara Boom, Clash Boom
       On a Sunday afternoon.
       Boom Bang Oompah Boom!

Fourth Episode: Old Age
—The Dance and the Night Procession—

Billy Belly's Boston Big Brass Band
Is playing for dances at the park's big bandstand.
Quicksteps, polkas, tangos, *and* . . . the waltz
Are on the program for tonight, 'cause Billy *loves* the waltz.
Well then, let us dance, let us dance Billy's waltz:
       One Two Three,
       Oom—Pah—Pah, Oom—Pah—Pah, *and* . . .
       One More Time:
       Oom—Pah—Pah, Oom—Pah—Pah, *and* . . .
So we waltz, and we dance, and we waltz.

Billy Belly's fine baton is surely like some magic wand,
For, look, he even makes grandma and grandpa dance
A quickstep, polka, tango, *and* . . . a waltz.
Each girl will find her boy tonight. Each boy will kiss his girl.
Well then, let us whirl, pretty girl, let us whirl:
       One Two Three,

Oom—Pah—Pah, Oom—Pah—Pah, *and* . . .
One More Time:
Oom—Pah—Pah, Oom—Pah—Pah, *and* . . .
So we whirl, and we twirl, and we whirl.

And so the dance and band go on and on
Until the dancers have enough of all those
Quicksteps, polkas, tangos, *and* . . . the waltz . . .
But before we call it a night and head for home,
We join the night procession with the Boston Band:

Cheeng—cheeng boom—
Torches, bright fantastic.
Shadows, music, magic . . .

Cheeng—cheeng boom—
Boston, light and dark.
Life, a passing spark . . .

Boom—boom cheeng—
Downtown fading away.
Starry sky till day . . .

Boom—boom cheeng—
Lonesome streets, Billy gone.
Life on earth goes on . . .

Cheeng—cheeng boom—
Far—off brass and lights.
Gentle sleep tonight . . .

Cheeng—cheeng boom—
Quiet, endless mirth.
Stars, heaven, earth . . .

Boom . . . Boom . . . Cheeng . . .

Great . . . Great . . . Great . . .

Olé, Bolero

A Fiesta in Sevilla

Glossary: *Olé* — bravo; *Bolero* — a Spanish dance; *fiesta* — festival; *gitanas* — female gypsies; *Sevilla* — a town in Spain; *Manzanilla* — a Spanish wine; *toreros* — bullfighters; *bravo* — shout of approval; *toro* — bull; *castanets* — hand percussion instruments; *¡Ay! ¡Ay! ¡Ay!* — exclamations of excitement; *matador* — bullfighter who kills the bull; *Seguidillas* — a Spanish dance; *Bulerías* — a Spanish dance; *Farruca* — a Spanish dance; *Cádiz* — a town in Spain; *arenas* — arenas; *guitarras* — guitars; *La Rosa* — female named Rosa; *pronto* — immediately; *La Carola* — female named Carola; *La Paloma* — female named Paloma; *siesta* — mid–day rest; *presto* — right away; *machismo* — masculine pride; *gusto* — enthusiasm; *España* — Spain

Part One: The Gitanas of Sevilla

Olé, Bolero, olé!
We are gitanas of beautiful, proud Sevilla.
We're fond of dancing, men, and Manzanilla.
Tonight we wait for handsome, famous toreros,
And after the bullfight, we'll dance the Bolero.
   Olé, Bolero. Bravo Toro!

   We play and click with our castanets
      And dream of all the men we soon will get.
   Olé, Bolero. *¡Ay! ¡Ay! ¡Ay!*, torero. Bravo Toro, bravo!
Meanwhile, we're dancing here and killing time,
   And each of us is scheming who'll be mine.
      So *I* will lure Eduardo and *I* for sure Carlitos,
         And *I'll* seduce José, and *I* will cruise Antonio.

Oh no, you won't, *or* you're dead before he ever sees your bed!
Oh yes, I will. I meant Antonio *Senior*—
      Ah, that's better, for *I'll* be seeing J*unior! ¡Ay! ¡Ay! ¡Ay!*
      Olé, Bolero. Olé, Toro, olé!
I think I'll get Juanito, and *I* will pet Pablito,
Well, *I* will *have* them *all*. But *I did* have them all. *¡Ay! ¡Ay! ¡Ay!*
      Olé, olé, toreros. Bravo Toro, olé!
         And *I* will tame their Matador!

Ha, tonight at the fiesta in Sevilla,
We first will dance the saucy Seguidillas,
And then the bouncy Bulerías, and then the foxy Farruca,
And if *that* doesn't cut it, we all
Will dance, dance the Bolero, the Bolero.
    Olé, olé, Bolero, olé! Bravo Toro! Bravo toreros, olé!

Part Two: The Toreros Visiting from Cádiz

    Olé, Bolero, olé!
We are toreros from ancient, noble Cádiz.
We're on our way to meet some classy ladies.
By day we fight for fame in Spanish arenas,
But oh, at night, we dance the Bolero.
    Olé, Bolero. Bravo Toro!

    We bring our daggers and fine guitarras
        And dream of wooing pretty gitanas.
    Olé, Bolero. ¡Ay! ¡Ay! ¡Ay!, gitana. Bravo Toro, bravo!
Each of us is hot and ready for action,
    And once we're there, *I* will *be* the attraction,
        So *I* will lead Carmencita, and *I* will meet Frasquita,
            And *I* will match Dolores, and *I* will catch La Rosa.

Oh no, you won't, or *I* will kill ya pronto on her bed in Sevilla!
Oh yes, I will. I meant the *daughter Rosita*—
    Ah, that's better, for *I* must have *la Madre!* ¡Ay! ¡Ay! ¡Ay!
    Olé, Bolero. Olé, Toro, olé!
All *I* need is La Carola. *I* would *die* for La Paloma—
But all would die for *me*. They *know* what *I* have *got*! ¡Ay! ¡Ay! ¡Ay!
        Olé, olé, gitanas. Bravo Toro, olé!
        And *I* will chase their sexy queen!

Ha, in sultry Sevilla after the siesta and bullfight,
We'll join the gitanas to dance and neck *all* night.
We'll drink Manzanilla, and play the guitarra,
And if *that* doesn't cut it, we all
Will dance, dance the Bolero, the Bolero.
    Olé, olé, Bolero, olé! Bravo Toro! Bravo gitanas, olé!

Part Three: The Dance at the Fiesta

Olé, Bolero, olé!
Ha, there they are, those handsome, famous toreros.
Let's have a sip of Manzanilla. Relax, toreros.
Sit down and have a chat with us now in Sevilla.
We'll dance, but first let's drink some Manzanilla.
Bravo Toro, bravo. Olé!

We're taking a break from bullfights in Cádiz.
Our daggers will charm you tonight, ladies.
Let's do it. Presto, bring more Manzanilla!
Let's have some music and dance in Sevilla.
Bravo Toro, bravo. Olé!

Now click your little castanets, gitanas. Olé, gitana,
Bewitch the toreros. Click, click, click. Olé, olé, olé.
Bravo castanets!
Now tune your fine guitarras, toreros. Olé, torero,
Enchant the gitanas. Play, play, play. Olé, olé, olé.
Bravo guitarras!

Now dance, Toro. Dance, dance the Bolero. Bravo Toro!
Ha, these toreros are champs at bullfights and dancing.
How well do they rule the arena of subtle romancing,
So gallantly treating the ladies, olé.

Now dance, Toro. Dance, dance the Bolero. Bravo Toro!
Ha, these gitanas, so neat at turning and bending in fashion.
How deftly they click and move with style and precision,
And yet they're wilder than toros in Cádiz, olé.

Left, gitana. Right, torero. Turn, torero. Bend, gitana.
Run, Toro, run the arena. What power, machismo and gusto—
Toreros from Cádiz, you've never been better.
Bravo Toro. Bravo toreros!
Ha, Carola. Ha, Pablito. Advance, Manolo. Retreat, Rosita.
Watch torero. Fight, Toro. What fervor, glamor and passion—
Sevillian gitanas, you're hotter than ever.
Bravo Toro. Bravo gitanas!

My bed your arena, torero. Olé, olé, Bolero.
My dagger is yours, gitana. Olé, olé, Bolero.
Thrust and dance, torero. Dance and yield, gitana.
Dance, Toro! Dance in Sevilla.

Dance, Edgardo, Alfredo, Roberto! *¡Ay! ¡Ay! ¡Ay!*
Dance, Maria, Alicia, Lucinda! *¡Ay! ¡Ay! ¡Ay!*
Viva Cádiz, Sevilla, España! *¡Ay! ¡Ay! ¡Ay!*
Dance, Toro. Dance, dance.

Viva La Rosa. Viva Rosita.
Bravo Senior. Bravo Junior.
Bravo, bravo Bolero.
Olé, Bolero,
Olé!

Calypso in Port of Spain, Trinidad

In Trinidad, Carlita once danced the calypso—
Never before have I seen such uh . . . hips!
In Port of Spain, Carlita once sang,
And nowhere have I kissed such uh . . . lips!
In her cozy home Carlita once
Danced and sang and *flaunted* her marvelous, shapely—
    Oh, calypso, calypso!
    Oh, Carlita, Carlita!
    You're driving me nuts, nuts, nuts,
    And I don't know why that is so,
    But I love you so, you and your uh . . .
Calypsos!

She took me home one night to show me some calypsos,
And there I learned much more of those uh . . . oops!
She showed me how great Trinidad is—
She's got those more than tempting uh . . . looks.
That night in Port of Spain, I clutched those—
I mean, that night I *touched* those marvelous, shapely—
    Oh, calypso, calypso!
    Oh, Carlita, Carlita!
    You're driving me nuts, nuts, coconuts,
    And *I* don't know why that is so,
    But I love you so, you and your uh . . .
Calypsos!

Next day, I called my boss to say I was sick or so—
Oh boy, if he knew how she was wiggling—
I wasn't sick at all in Trinidad—
And then on top of me, why she was giggling!
I was just snugly lying down in Port of Spain
When she was *shaking* for me her marvelous, shapely—
    Oh, calypso, calypso!
    Oh, Carlita, Carlita!
    You're driving me nuts— You're driving me coco—
    You're driving me C O C O — N U TS, NUTS, NUTS!
    And I don't know why that is so,
    But I love you so, you and your uh . . .
Calypsos!

FIRE DANCE

A Tribal Invocation of the Light

Glow, fire, glow.
Whisper, crackle, shimmer.
Grow, fire, grow, grow.
Sparkle, illumine, glimmer.
Soar, fire, soar.
Reach higher, higher. Dance!
Illumine, illuminate, oh luminous fire.
Illuminate, oh Goddess, illumine us all.
We kindle the fire and once every year,
in the night of surrender,
we gather to worship the Goddess in secret
with magic, fire, and dance
by the radiant light on the face of the moon.

Singe, fire, singe.
Glisten, hiss and sizzle.
Leap, fire, leap, leap.
Radiate, scintillate, dazzle.
Dance, fire, dance.
Go higher, higher. Shine!
We've chosen the virgin. Her eyes are fire.
Enliven, oh virgin, enliven us all.
We're painted all over in screaming colors.
We glow like embers.
We glitter, gleaming at night,
and tremble in front of the Goddess of fire and doom
by the terrible light on the face of the moon.

Rage, fire, rage!
Soar and glisten. Roar.
Blaze, fire, blaze, blaze.
Fill us with luster. Soar.
Intenser, intenser. Burn.
Shine, fire, shine brighter!
Encircle, oh fire, encircle us all.
We glare and pant and growl. Nothing will stop us,

43

and from the bottom of the pit,
and out of the blackest of shadows, the devils arise
to revel in row after row with the ghosts of the dead,
and slowly a cloud of sulphur and dread
enshrouds the face of the moon.

Glare, fire, glare.
Beat, drummers, beat.
The witch doctor screams!
The sounds of hundreds of
pounding bare feet on the ground
and hammering fists and knuckles on drums
rebound and cut through the jungle around us,
engulfing, enthralling, ensnaring us all.
We watch an inferno and dance like demons—
the virgin screams!
We prance and growl, completely in trance;
we shake and crawl to the Goddess
and sprawl by the light of flaming surrender and fire.

Burn, fire, burn.
Roast and blister. Scorch.
The spirits of fire
squirm and dance on pyre and torch.
As the moon reappears,
we pray for redemption and
dash to the flames to fearlessly dance on the coals.
We cleanse ourselves. Each soul is redeemed.
The sacrificed blood of the virgin is boiled.
The scent appeases the nostrils of Her,
the Goddess of fire, and reaches to all of the stars
in the vault of the sky by the blood red light
on the face of the moon.

Glow, fire, glow.
And now we lie down by the fire to dream.
Glow, fire, glow.
Life is a dream,
a brittle illusion. When is it real?
Glow, fire, glow.

Before we know, life will be over.
Glow, surround us, oh, fire, envelop us all.
And light will brighten each feature.
Warmth will kindle each heart. The glow
of stars will show the heavenly eyes
of the Goddess of fire on high by the light
on the luminous face of the moon.

Great Goddess of fire,
soaring higher, higher.
Who has beheld
your splendor and lived?
Oh Goddess, radiant, vibrant and bright.
We're awed by your grandeur.
Your eyes are millions of stars. Your face
is the sky all ablaze, igniting us all.
Your essence now fills our being.
We love and adore you.
At last we come to ourselves to laugh,
to sing and to reel. The sky is a witness to joy
by the glorious light on the face of the moon.

Sing, fire, sing.
The light of the stars
has touched our souls.
The children come forward with
garlands, palm leaves, and fruits.
Sing, fire. Sing, dance.
Illumine, illuminate, oh magical fire.
Illuminate, oh Spirit, illumine us now.
We chant with angels, seraphs, and gods.
We're sinless and free.
We rise to the One, the highest of all.
We dwell in ourselves, and we know, and we bow
to the glimmering light in the east, to the dawn . . .

Glow, fire, glow.
And here comes the dawn,
the mystical dawn.
Rise, fire, rise over death.

And here comes the sun, the glorious sun.
Today is the day of peace and surrender.
We rise from the shadows. We rise from the night.
We look to the East. We reach for the Light.
Oh Light, oh all-seeing Light,
eternal, boundless, loving and bright.
Illumine, illuminate, oh all-knowing Light.
Illumine, illuminate, ignite now, oh Light.
Ignite the spark that has lived and endured in us all.

THE BOMB THAT
BLEW UP GOD

VOLCANOES

Erupt they will,
like Krakatoa exploded over Indonesia
and Mount Vesuvius blasted away Pompeii.

Cracked open wide,
volcanoes speak with fury, lava, smoke,
exposing explosive truths, dishonest debris.

Eruptions launch
earthquakes, tsunamis, revelations,
affirming a seismic, urgent shift in us all.

Earth will burn,
Vulcan, god of volcanoes roars, and
seething blood will boil for days and nights on end.

"The world will change,"
young Bolsheviks, Blacks, and French Revolutionaries chant,
their jawbones groaning aloud in countless tongues.

Long-held secrets
will soon be ripped to shreds in the streets,
halls of power, and hideouts of tyrants.

The Earth Mother
fiercely rises with seers, artists,
and icons as Gandhi, King, Mandela, forging ahead.

Erupt will all,
as hellbent scientists, workers, students,
multitudes, continents, and worlds of rage most certainly will.

The truth will out,
the Elders cry, raising the soul of the land,
and Mankind, battered and shaken, finally listens.

CLAUSTROPHOBIA OF AN AFTERNOON

Those large, rectangular slabs of cement
in the parking lot can make you feel trapped
longer than the instant you notice them
on stepping out of your car.

Soon you walk into narrow, endless corridors
to hit square slabs of linoleum in cramped
waiting rooms; vast parquets in malls, shops,
and offices where smallish windows frame the
outside sphere of light you came from and
may not return to in time.

Angular tables await you, cold chairs,
dressers, sharp countertops — stuck like you in
interminable spaces of useless thought,
and your vision becomes narrow like
the width of your very eye.
Walls, floors, ceilings high and low are waiting to
cave and box you in; flatten you from all sides,
mocking your panting to find a way to escape.

How you long for those open spaces
arching over cities day and night;
abundant arcs of pure sky; rare rainbows, clouds;
anything circular, spherical — the sun, the moon;
a face, a soul, a circle of friends;
the ball you played with as a kid,
the globe, orbits, galaxies.
Your recurring thoughts turn to
the exact same thoughts as yesterday's —
trapped as you are in stale ideas,
cut off from true expansion,
living in templates not serving you at all.

Images of squares, streets and a measure of living
you can still recall — hallways, staircases, rooms
where windows one after another close shut fast,
showing less and less of the light you
were taking for granted year after year;
and swiftly now the blinds come down,
obscuring the spherical, bright world
you wish to return to, to step into the distant,
shimmering plazas of sunshine once again,
before getting back to your car,
although it may be caked with dirt by now,
or hauled away long ago . . .

Sound Barrier

When that sudden jet went crashing,
Boom! Boom! Boom!
through the sound barrier a second ago,
it struck me how so many
sound ideas—once left unuttered;

never expressed; perhaps
never-brought-up-anymore;
then left behind,
or silenced (I'm afraid) forever—
are now rearing their angry heads again,

cursing at this hopelessness
larger than any sky
where frantic echoes keep banging,
Damn! Damn! Damn! inside my skull,
and I'm cringing here right now,

knowing how often I wanted to really
speak up for myself,
feeling so damn motivated,
but then suddenly
couldn't, couldn't, couldn't . . .

Statue of an Enraged Lion

I saw an angel in the stone and carved to set it free.
    —Michelangelo

Who condemned your savage spirit to stone
and chiseled your features—then left you alone?
He squashed your pride, but as you hardly age,
your stony hide expands with noble rage.

Your mighty roar is now a marble cry,
but hell, you won't give up—you'd rather die!
How many lifetimes have you wished him hell?
To hell he'll go—your bulging eyes can tell.

He left you with that anger in your eye,
but if you won't unleash your wrath and try
to tear this hulking shape apart to rise
triumphant from your bitter years in stone,
how will you beat his arrogant renown
and grasp what lions would consider wise?

DOWNFALL

Scheming behind their walls of
secrecies, lies and politics,

they decide what's right or wrong
for us, the common people.

That's what they're good at: dividing us
and getting away with that.

Around a darkening globe, a few
sane minds still shine,

but as light begins to wane
where truth was choked and brushed aside,

a deeper night now falls, and
wrong usurps what's right.

REALMS OF STONE

These are the hidden realms of stone and
light where we're fiercely on our own,
but for now I'll wander about the lawn,
enjoy the trees, the grass, the people.
These are no times for weak knees or
hiding our heads with ostriches from truth.
The mire and quicksand are too deep already;
I know the darn routine — I'm involved.

The summer grass gives under my tread and
flattens out wherever I step on it,
yet it is resilient, curving back without
much effort while the years grow sparse.
An unsubtle rumble of thunder lurks
above the elms this bright, cloudless day.

Where have our senses and seasons gone?
Slipped underneath the grass with water after
a drizzle? But doesn't last week's rain
collect between earth crust and rock bed?
A late sunlight blazes all over the place
alongside countless, aimless shadows. We're
doomed to bridge these vast, unwelcome times
to reach some quiet corners in our lives.

The calm identity of grass seems to be all we
have beside some smatterings of light. But *no!*—
mere comfort isn't enough. I'm calling for the
shine on solid stone that I will hone before the
great blur kicks in, and trees, grass, rocks
and Mankind roll away with histories of stars.

THE BOMB THAT BLEW UP GOD

A Fable — The True History of the Big Bang

The Devil insisted on having the latest, baddest
bombs tested, but God wasn't thrilled, so
Satan flew over to Heaven, smirking and hissing,
"You know that *my* army is much, much
larger than Yours, and You are opposing *Me?*"
God glared and said, "Hell, yes! Those bombs
are the worst, and you know it." "So,"
Satan replied, "and whose fault is that? You
created Adam and Eve!" God sighed,
"You talk back too much. Go back to Hell."
God retired and Angels sang Him to sleep.

Livid, the Devil went down to Hell, but soon
concocted a masterly, truly hellish plan.
He went over to see the smartest, scariest
scientists around and said, "Make me a bomb
that will blow up almighty God." Even though
being roundly shocked, they went to work at
once. They'd always been secretly smitten
with Satan's shenanigans anyway. After
splitting some newly discovered particles,
they called the Devil, "We did it. Come on
over. It's all yours." Satan didn't wait long.

Overjoyed, he picked up ten bombs, just in
case; dashed in a flash to Heaven; snuck past
the Angels into God's bedroom, and put a
bomb smack under His bed. God was taking a
nap. Satan snickered, "Sweet dreams," and,
boom, blew up God! And *everything* blew up:
Creation, Heaven, Man, the Universe, All.
The only realm remaining was all hell.
Satan lit up, roaring with laughter, and cried,
"Ha, now I can finally play with bombs as long
as I please and bomb the hell out of Hell."

And so he did. He dropped bomb after bomb
on Hell, blowing up mega zillions of souls.
At last, after killing everyone, he sat down on
one last, functional bomb in Hell and boomed,
"Now *I'll* create, for I AM GOD!" And that did it:
the bomb blew up him! From that time on,
nothing, absolutely nothing remained . . . but
God woke up and said, "Do you see now what
I mean?" and started Creation one more time,
but Satan had an even more devilish plan.
God knew, and never, never slept again . . .

THESE THREE WORDS

There are three words wrestling to be
heard above the thunder and terror of
World War Three.

They're simple and good, and
understood at once by each of us:
Peace, love, joy.

Despite bombs, scattered remains, and
endless pains, these three words endure:
Peace, love, joy.

And so it is, and may we regain what
it was we all heard once, clear as a bell:
These three words.

A Dove in Times of War

1

A sudden sense of peace
on everything . . . What's that daring creature
on the wing?

Something hovering
finds a nest . . . and gracefully gliding
comes to rest.

An atmosphere of change
ruffles the air . . . The quiet dove of peace
is settling there.

2

I guess I am aware, unlike
this homing pigeon, that one more war around
the world is raging,

but maybe doves abide in spheres
devoid of strife, and may not see how *we* can live
a warring life.

How odd: this fleeting scene
instills somehow the age-old archetype of peace
in Man who kills and kills.

3

I fear we can't avert
these constant wars, but let's appreciate how
enduring metaphors

descend unasked sometimes
and give us pause to fathom our crushing bent
for war, because

right here's the paradox:
eventually all of Mankind *sees* this lovely dove
and quiet air at peace.

BRIDGE UNDER CONSTRUCTION

1

See how those two blunt ends
so eagerly reaching out,
change into one fine bridge.

2

See them becoming friends
sharing constant traffic
bonding their bare wrists.

An Upside-Down World

There's an upside-down world most of you
know little about. The upside-down cake was
invented up here, but someone took the recipe
down one day so you could have it. Too bad
there isn't more you remember from this place
where life is being lived never feeling blue.

Please, come on up sometime and see how we
turn the ups and downs of life into the ups and ups.
Quite often we wish you'd visit, you know. You
see, if you were feeling down, you'd get upbeat
in seconds. We've had people's high blood
pressure going down in a whoosh for sure. Try it.

If you visit long enough, you'll have a good chance
to become even-keeled and start appreciating
what *what's up* really means. But if you think to
come here to flaunt your ego, talking down
to others, you'll be in for quite a shock. *You* will
be talking *up*, praising *them* to high heaven.

Once you get over that, you'll start feeling
quite at home, I promise. At least we all hope you
will. Come have a look at our upside-down ways,
our habits, pleasures; why we chose to be here;
where we're going, and why we think we've got
the real deal without being uppity about it.

Oh, but you want to know about our sex life, right?
How we do it? Well, angels we ain't—we multiply,
but what do you wanna hear—you, who already
know the *Kama Sutra* backward? Oh? The up and
down part? Well, what if the apple Eve dropped
bounced up before Adam got down to business?

We flipped over; *Mankind* fell. Once you get used to
loafing upside-down, you'll figure it out. But let's
have some upside-down cake now. You'll find it goes
up well. Logic never went down well up here, but
you'll be fine; you won't throw up—see how healthy we
look? The bottom line: we beat gravity and live it up.

We've got here all you'll ever need. We love to share,
and have resolved such opposites like war and peace,
good and bad. *Impossible*, you say? Not so! Long ago
we tossed the '*im*' of *im-possible* to make such things
possible. Welcome to our upside-down world.
Here, take my hand and just flip over. You'll see.

The Tool

What if I dared to be called a fool by some,
but stuck to what felt right for me, if not for them...?

Sometimes the gods may choose domestic ways
to quietly reveal the depth of what they want to say.

One day, something trying to peek out of the dirt
set me wondering about its shape and likely girth.

An edge was all that showed above the soil. It gave
no clue to me as yet of what it did not have.

I nudged the top somewhat. It was a broken spade.
I dug it out and grabbed its firm, though rusty blade.

Would I, without a handle on it, then go dig around
to find a missing handle matching it, if ever found?

Although this thing could still be used, it was no tool.
If I went on, would people watching think I was a fool?

I couldn't handle this, nor could I leave and let it lie,
and what good is a tool without a grip to hold it by?

I dug some more with what I'd found to shift the sand,
and hid it then for good. I used my own bare hands,

and after I was done, I finally came to understand
why Nature left no tool for me but shaped a hand.

SPRING PICK UP

Tired, old washing machines and dryers;
ragged sofas, broken chairs;
matresses with or without bed bugs;
dead branches; clutter from the basement;
trite 'collectibles', and trash bags full of junk
line the curbs in town for two full weeks.

Scavengers in pickup trucks drive slowly by,
ready to haul away most anything,
and yet keenly look for whatever still might
be fixable, presentable and possibly sold
in some far away state, or perhaps kept.

The town is ready for its spring facelift
and eager to get rid of what is old.
We're looking for *stuff*, even if not great stuff
but good enough to use when cleaned,
repaired, painted over, and all of it for free.

In no time, before the 'City' comes round
to do it officially, the town
will be picked clean like a camel
dead two weeks in the Sahara, while
we're all busy getting cluttered again with
'*new*' old junk for pick up in a spring or two.

A ZEBRA MOMENT

1

It's what you don't see
what often matters most.

2

Today, a zebra slowly
crossed a zebra crossing,
becoming invisible
for just a split second
as the striped pavement
aligned with its stripes.

3

What a perfect moment
of stillness all over town,
simply making you see
the unexpected right here.
The whole cosmos stopped
on the spot for one zebra.

4

And suddenly all traffic
races round the sun again.

BIRTHPLACE

He who loves his native home
where all his fathers lived and died—
he is never far from home.

He who hums his native songs,
remembered from his mother's lips—
he still treasures all her songs.

He can hear them word for word,
although he left his native land
without goodbye, without a word.

He who cares to come back home
where all of us remember him—
he now feels his heart come home,

for here he treads his fathers' land
where we, his kin, reside. Replete
with tears he greets his dearest land.

VIGNETTES

AFFLUENCE

To make both ends meet,
you need at least two ends.
To handle two ends, you surely
need at least one beginning.

For that, you want some room,
and there, over time, we'll find
a meeting place of minds,
people, lives, ideas, friends.

It'll take at least two of those
to make things happen. To have
us connect, let's meet now.
In the end we'll strike it rich.

A Marriage

After the shouting,
the insults,

the barely suppressed tears
and five days apart,

there's the meeting
and slow smile,

the shy kiss exchanged
and half open doorway.

LIFESPAN OF A HAIKU

irresistibly forming
formally finished
this haiku begins
ends

Cloudburst

furious windshield wipers
ditto rain   no.   worse:
can't see a thing dammit

Nose Haiku

Picking my nose,
hoping nobody notices
how much I like it.

Broken Toy

broken toy I can't fix
we are poor
my son sobbing can't sleep

On the Sidewalk

flies abruptly scatter
as my huge hurried foot
almost hits a turd

Twenty Dollar Bill

a swirling twenty dollar bill
my foot goes
tap—tap—wham—gotcha

On a Medieval Painting of the Fall of Man

The Angel turned them out of Paradise,
And God withdrew within.
A glorious Realm receded from their Eyes.
They shrank from loving Him.

The World is like a Darker Sphere until
We meet His Love within.
An Angel full of Grace is waiting still
To lead us back to Him.

A History of Sarcasm

Stuck as I was in a
shady history of
sarcasm far too long,
I decided at last to
shut up and not play
the bully anymore.

Lo and behold:
I watched meanness
flowing down chasms
carved centuries ago
I have no need to
cling to anymore.

THE LOVESICK ANEMONE

Anemone Japonica (Anemone hybrida x)

1

A discarded anemone floating on a pond
languishes beneath the shadow of a pagoda.

Pondering over its reflection and towering
to the starry sky, the pagoda scarcely
notices the anemone.

The pond, forever serene, gently lets
the flower drift away out of the shadow.

2

A woman stoops by the brink of the pond,
picks up the anemone and takes it home.

She puts it in a bowl of water by her bed
for her lover to notice in case he should
want to meet again.

The pond gazes at stars with the pagoda's
long shadow glimmering through the night.

Looking Out the Window in Autumn

The window shares a vista:
     A tree against the sky—
Branches, bare like winter—
     The air, a patch of gray—
A maze of twigs in a haze
     And hasty passersby
With autumn on each face.

Silent Question

That drunk at the bar
was looking to talk again,
he who so ardently once
had rambled on, and on,
preaching peace on earth.

I wasn't sober either, but
looking away, thinking
about drunks. No thoughts
about peace today, just
trying not to drink much.

Yet his glance seemed
sincere somehow,
but how to fancy peace
on earth without a
bottle full to live it?

LETTERS IN A DRAWER

better-forgotten memories
and long-held hopes,
remembered all too well
from this cranky,
so familiar handwriting

unforgotten, unforgiving

A Bird Landing

Wildly fluttering and
balancing on air,

a bird
about to pertly
perch someplace,
its feet stretched out
to touch down fast,

suddenly drops,

lands.

FINESSE

She was a French and easy beauty,
seductive with plenty of *that!*
Flaunting some legs, 'n this, 'n that,
she practiced with art and
obvious ease
her ample, horizontal,
upfront . . . finesse.

He was an older, eager sucker,
loaded with dollars galore.
He sported cars, cigars, cash,
and hunted all night
for hot and willing flesh,
displaying thrilling, financial
ease, and . . . excess.

They met, of course, in gay Paree.
She wanted glitter, dresses, mink.
He ogled for hot, opulent pink!
They settled for *these*,
and both were deeply pleased
with panting, well-earned ease,
and slick . . . success.

Sunset Blues

I guess these are my lesser days.

I'm wondering what's been going on.
A carefree, sunny time has gone.

What's left is neither this nor that.
The sun is low; my life seems set,

yet much is still unsaid, not done,
and who will care when I am gone?

The sky's all red with lesser rays.

A Breakup

Sun in the park . . .
on your hand
on the bench
on your set face.

Shadows below . . .
by *my* feet,
by *your* feet,
by that bench.

One pair of feet goes
east, one west . . .
One fading image
stays . . . That bench.

NIGHT SECRET

Deep in the night between lovers,
there's a secret
sent down from Heaven:

All romantic love ends in suffering,
one way or other.
Only God's love lives on.

Behold now these two:
Holding on to His love
they rise despite their tears.

THE TOUCH

Vaguely, from the dark cave of night
when my dream was still at its height,
I felt a soft touch that lingered . . .

Was that your hand on my fingers?
But before I found the time to say,
"My love?" I woke upon this lonely day.

FIREWORKS

pow, ka-BOOOOM, fizzzz.
yellow — pink — green — ahhh,
and behind all that emotion:
endless eternities of stars...

My Daddy's Hands

When I, a little baby boy, was reaching for
my father's huge index finger, I didn't know
what I'm now starting to remember:
that daddy was beyond happy.

But there came a time of misconceptions
and later, rage; tears shed, but in the
open only once. Late came the hour
I could've held his old, beautiful hands.

My hands never resembled his, except
for my index finger and thumb. His gently
playing with my tiny, tiny finger lives on
beyond the years in my own empty hands.

DO WE REALLY DIE

AUTUMN IN A CEMETERY

The trees about the graves still wear their summer crown,
but autumn gales are out to strip their branches down,
and all along the walks, the leaves dropped like the dead
who went one day to meet their deep, terrestrial bed.

The mighty breath of God is heard throughout the sky,
and all day long these leaves are blown to where we lie,
but as they find a resting place like we did once,
their lives are only spent till spring — not so is Man's.

You countless leaves, how strange it is to find you here
but know that you'll be back reborn another year
when all of you return, pretty much looking the same,
to grow on trees again while we're becoming a name.

This eerie time between extremes of summer heat
and chilling cold, where wind, and leaf and Man now meet
is but a ghostly realm where Death lies now alone,
yet life should *live* — not be immovable like stone!

A whirl among the foliage finds a futile chance
to flaunt above the somber walks a fitful dance.
But all the storms we one time knew have had their will,
and soon mere nothingness will rule where all is still.

A frosty air is settling all around the place,
and even leaves won't move at all in coming days,
and where they cover graves and all, there is not one
that hasn't fallen mute like all the dead of Man.

Deep snow will blanket all of us until the spring
when life awakens trees, and birds come nest and sing.
But here we breathe a troubled air and do not die
until we know the ultimate, eternal why...

FALLING TREE KILLS SLEEPING CUB SCOUT

Monday, June 7, 2004 GARDNERS, Pennsylvania (AP)
A 40-foot pine tree fell in a state park, killing a
7-year-old Cub Scout sleeping in a tent.
—For Owen Ryberg Lentz, 1996—2004

It made headlines on the news today—
One bright kid, so eager to learn about Nature
and how to live in harmony with Her,
dreaming in a tent, looking forward to tomorrow's
challenges. One brief moment of
timeless living . . . and Nature called him home.

June 7, 2004

By a Pond

1

A swan took flight on rustling wings.
      The setting sun reflects upon a pond.
      Hear the evening silence widening.

I sense the slow beat of my
      heart, and there's a sudden quiet
      present, spreading everywhere.

2

The swan is gone. I ponder on my
      lingering, earthly existence
      slowly drawing to a close, yet here I am.

What's keeping me here? This lonely
      heart? Its persistence? My passion?
      Swan, where then did you go?

3

A man stood up, turned around, left.
      Far from here, in the bustle of cities, he
      recalls how hope rose high one noon;

how a far silence overwhelmed him;
      how a shadow slanted past his face,
      and his future swiftly winged away.

RUN OVER PIGEON

But what if I'd
never seen that pigeon
and carried on, not facing my deep fears of death?

I almost stepped on it:
a dead pigeon —
beak crushed — wings spread — flattened on the road.

My heart stopped cold —
I felt
my blood draining — no life left — squashed.

I stepped over it, eyeing
it sideways,
my heart pounding with impending death.

TO THE SUN

A secret, lifelong infatuation with the sun,
taking me on inner journeys
unknown to anyone but myself,
is still my untold joy.

Facing south here in my sun room,
taking an alert snooze is one of my
favorite pastimes. Light
catches my body at its very best, creative!

Next to that—believe it or not—I like to sleep
which I usually do
in my room to the east. The
early morning rays become all mine.

Four short blocks north of here
sits my favorite grocery store. There
I buy my veggies, fruit, rice, and
anything the sun ever nurtured and caressed.

Returning home from shopping,
I cross the railroad track which runs
straight west. I've seen gorgeous sunsets there
giving me much to think about.

Edging toward the so-called sunset
of my life, I sometimes wonder:
Was it not like yesterday
that I, standing tall in broad daylight;

my feet firmly planted to the earth;
my arms stretched out
wide like a tree; my crown
reaching out to that deep, wonderful sky,

when I ecstatically asserted myself:
I'm here, yes, here. Touch me,
it's me, all me, me; look at me:
Freddy, Freddy, head to toe, heart and soul?

I may have passed the zenith of earthly life—
the sun out there can tell,
always tracking me down anywhere
in the north, south, east, or west.

But in my sun room, lying down,
reveling in the warm embrace
of today, my ailing frame still basks, plans,
chipper as ever,

and I'm all centered here, catching these
late, slanting rays shifting westward,
passing my window onto other
continents and newer times . . .

CROSSING A BRIDGE DURING A TIDAL WAVE

Across this long, long bridge,
cars are madly speeding with just one thought:
faster, faster, before everything collapses!

You floor it or die. The end is near.
There won't be any words to describe it
other than language corpses tell.

I may not be able to make it.
The water is too close already, and yes,
I'm now riding on the long, long wave home.

Where will the car be found, if at all?
Unrecognizably shattered in the hinterlands?
But that swollen body...was that there me?

GENERATIONS

I

Funeral services are being held at church across the street
again.
I've no idea who died. I'm just walking by.

II

A loud bunch of kids is playing on the sidewalk.
Oh such
happy shrieks and hollers ringing all over the place!

III

Play, kids, play, the future is yours still and *should* be,
until
you're walking by one day maybe, and not know me either.

FALLING DOWN A MANHOLE

A manhole in the sidewalk,
tunneling down all the way to the
center of Earth it seems,
and I, breathlessly
tumbling down at dizzying speed,
making no bones about my ultimate
and sure fate.

The further down I go, the more lost
I become while unstoppably crashing
down a greasy ladder,
my ears barely getting
used to the sharp
whoosh cutting off my breath,
down, down to where
there is suddenly
all peace.

AFTER A SWIM

There comes a time in the affairs
of man when he must take the bull
by the tail and face the situation.
                              —WC Fields

Inside the shark's belly,
it's really a bit too late
to worry much whether
I locked my front door
before going swimming.

I'm sure I'm marked as
missing now, but despite
my having gotten chopped
into many different parts
before getting swallowed
live, I still have all my keys
rattling in my swimsuit
in case the shark finds
I'm not eatable after
all and spits me out.

Reaching for my key now,
I'm swimming to my door,
but where on earth
did my right hand go?

DEAD FLY BY THE WINDOW

Dead fly,
you broke your wings against the window pane.
You died in sight of life, but
      freed from woe.

Frantic
was your aim, mistaking window glass
for air and sun and trees and
      life on earth.

Dead fly,
you broke your wings against the window pane.
Your soul flew thru the glass and
      dropped what dies.

DARK POND

A Night Piece

It was a night of unheard-of quiet
in some remote park

where shadows of dark, leafy trees
rested on a calm pond.

The faint fragrance of summer's end
still hung in the air.

No branch ever stirred. The world
had ceased to exist.

What somber question hovered there
below the

sable weight of night, shrouding my
being, my life, me?

In *that* vast silence it felt so right
to die alone . . .

But how on earth could I have faced
my final hour?

Had there been a bird call,
instead of that silent omen,

I could've lain down in peace and
somehow braved

the dark calm of fading dreams . . .
But no, I ducked in fear when,

rushing out of nowhere, that sudden
strange, dark *shape* flitted past;

and ever since I fled the pond's brink,
a mute, unspeakable *something*

has remained . . .
untold . . .

THREE TREES IN CENTRAL PARK

Three trees,
one of them: the one on the left
may be dying now,
its bare branches looking
awfully cracked and lonely.

The one in the middle,
still braving
a crisp, autumnal glow—
only a few streaks of crimson
in mostly still fantastic green.

The third one an evergreen.
It won't change much
in days to come,
although snow will be pressing down
a branch or two.

I sense a sudden kinship
with things eternal,
life, death, birth.
How stirring to watch these three
trees in a row in Central Park.

STRANGE RENEWAL

THE LANGUAGE OF THE FUTURE

If I ever turn into a real poet,
let it be of ever-evolving language—
that human, intangible, phenomenon
evoking poems, rivers, worlds and God,
taking you and me
...to the future.

Such a prospect will boldly reunite
the denizens and builders of
all languages past and present. One language,
more fluent than rivers we know, will
manifest, maturing in time
...in our future.

The language of the future will flow
with newfound ideas straight from God,
and thus will we sing and speak as One. I'll
keep my wit vibrant, making sure my
every word reaches for
...that grand future.

Looking at the Taj Mahal

Let the splendor of diamond, pearl and ruby vanish.
Only let this one teardrop, this Taj Mahal,
glisten spotlessly bright on the cheek of time, forever and ever.
—Rabindranath Tagore

The fanfare over the beauty of the Taj Mahal
is sometimes a bit much. Who on earth doesn't
know it from photos, postcards, books, the Internet
already? Legend has it that when you get there
to see it the first time, you're going to be completely
overwhelmed, to say the least—and yet, I'm not
so sure of that. Haven't I seen famous landmarks
on TV before, but when visiting one, wasn't it
just like getting sucked into a photograph? To me
it always felt like déjà-vu and over-familiarity
closing in on me, trivializing what I was looking
at. Would it be any different at the Taj Mahal?

I'm almost there and quickly getting pulled into
the dizzying perspective racing towards the
elegant, gleaming, seemingly weightless, marble
structure of the mausoleum, and deep into an
endless distance beyond the skyline of the slender
minarets set against the vast blue sky of India.
Intensely bright sunlight bounces about the
colossal, central dome shooting all of the light
straight back to where it came from. Flanked by
wide walkways leading towards the base of the
Taj Mahal, the long canals spectacularly mirror its
symmetry in a clear, upside-down view of grandeur.

My doubts are being instantly lifted on taking in the
vista. The color of the sky in India surpasses the
mere synthetic blue you see on photos, satisfying
my craving for reality. Frankly, this distant splendor
that I can't put my finger on is driving me almost
crazy now, because what I'm looking at is only a
beautifully framed, neat poster of the Taj Mahal on a

103

wall at India Cafe on Burlington where I'm waiting
to be served. In fact, I'm thinking: What if I completely
forgot photographs; pushed all frames out of the way;
stepped into the full sunshine of India; walked up to
the Taj Mahal in real time, and looked for myself at

this one teardrop, this Taj Mahal,
glistening spotlessly bright on the cheek of time,
forever and ever?

LONG-LOST BOOKS

long-lost books
on shelves of
friends,

long-forgotten

THE SAHARA

A Spiritual Journey

I

Sahara, Sahara,
empty, vast, untamable Sahara!
While your waving dunes evoke an ocean rolling
to some unknown shore, a giant nothingness
defines your deadly, desert plains.

II

From the valleys of the Nile way east
towards the far Atlantic coast, and from
the Atlas Mountains in the north, stretches your immense
domain, encroaching on the dry Sahel and sparse
Sudan savannas further south.

III

Aided by a scorching sun
and drought, unbearable, your fingers
spread in tongues of streaming fire. Perhaps never
will you return what lands you've seized and added
to your arid, desolate realm.

IV

Who knows how many empires
once were trampled here beneath your stride?
You've been relentless, and your heat is still a cruel hell,
for even Death is crawling wasted on your parched,
deserted lap . . . alone!

V

Yet far away some caravans
emerge . . . Slow, like pilgrims from the past, tracking
age-old routes, they come and go across your shifting soil
to find perhaps a short-lived respite, mere mirage,
or steady goal . . .

VI

Saharan sandstorms loom.
who is yearning, wailing in the desert there and barely
stumbling forward? How long will he stay blinded by
a force unseen where sunlight hasn't pierced
as yet his soul?

VII

Caravans, caravans
braving horror, loneliness, and death,
a haven lies ahead of you, if not a perfect
paradise, shimmering like some far-off island calling
from a desert sea.

VIII

Oasis, oasis,
splendid, green and lush oasis!
Beyond the gulfs of thirst in the Sahara, you beam
forever in a trembling drop of hope before the loving,
outspread arms of God . . .

IX

Paradise, Paradise,
sacred, newfound Paradise;
eternal source of youth and immortality.
One day I knelt before your well, and ages fell away
and sank into the sand.

X

Precious water, precious life,
gleaming in this fine oasis like some
brilliant diamond encased. The thirst that seemed
unquenchable is quenched at last, and Heaven rests
reflected on your face.

XI

I've seen the desert changing
through the years, and as I pause with outspread arms
in my oasis, all the hopeless,
erstwhile nothingness once surrounding my existence
rolls now far away . . .

AFTER READING AN OBSCURE VOLUME
OF UNUSUAL POETRY

Unbearably fierce, yet hauntingly beautiful are the two extremes
of this dark poetry,
relentlessly rushing, an angry river cleaving unsung forests
of passionate pain.

All those raw terms, driving rhythms, ballsy metaphors,
so full of the angst of our Age,
finally flow into an ocean of questions unanswered after my
reading the very last line.

Turning to a blank page, I feel like a river scanning the horizon,
searching for meaning.
Is this outlandish work's purpose meant to drown, or save us?
Is chaos beauty?

And yet, in some shared emotion, the poet and I embrace
this volume's timely content.
Together we lift this sad Earth high to let a gentle sunlight dry
her age-old, bitter tears.

Nocturnal Squeaks

Almost falling asleep evokes wonder,
but when, at night, the house
relaxes its construction with odd, sudden
bangs downstairs, or quirky snaps and
squeaks in corners or behind a wall,
I'm not always that relaxed,
since I'm still hearing
all of that and not falling
asleep.

Here's my breathing. There's a
loud churning gurgling in my
belly, too. I turn one more time.
The bed starts groaning, the
linen loudly crinkling about my
hopelessly alert body.
My patient pillow
sharply whizzes, crackling against
my ear.

Do houses talk to people they
shelter? Do they address
our secrets, idiosyncrasies, dreams?
A house may shield us from untold
fears, but why does its nightly presence
make us feel so vulnerable,
and what are we to a house?
Questions, questions all night long, and I am
still awake . . .

I will drift off at some point, but
deeper mysteries remain . . . I wonder:
Will the house keep squeaking
all night long, or is there
some gentle presence looming
over my bed now like Mom
long ago, adjusting the covers,
then tiptoeing away reassured,
unheard?

On Reading That 'The Atlantic Monthly' Has a Backlog of Poetry Submissions of 6-12 Months and Receives Some 50,000 Poems a Year, but Poetry Editor Peter Davison Responds in Three Weeks, and How He Does That

A Play in One Act

To shred or not to read, that's the question.
—Willie Jack Spear

Yes, please
come on in. You are the new girl?
Please check on that order for more rejection slips.
Not in yet? Oh God, look at all those stacks here. Get me the
shredder:
　　　　Plan B.
　　Why sir?
We're way behind schedule, that's why,
and heaps of poems keep coming in. Some poets
re-send their rejects all the time. Gonna be busy, so please no
calls.
　　　　What's next?
　　Oh boy,
more experimental drivel—must've been written
backward. Arrgh, ten pages of avant-garde and no substance?
Playing how abstruse you can get? Wasting my time, huh? There . . .
　　　　Shreds it.
　　Haiku,
five of them . . . always a quick
read, thank you God. Seven sonnets on love, oh Lordy. Petrarchan,
too. At least some substance, a rarity these days. The grammar stinks.
　　　　Shreds them.
　　Hm, what's
This one now: Coffee Stains On My Best Poem!
Now *there's* a title for you. Shit, there *are* coffee stains on it.
Fits the bill. Debby, would you get me some coffee, please. Milk,
no sugar.

Shreds it.
        Dring! Dring!
Please, I'm busy. Trying to keep up with the
future of poetry here. Gawd, how am I gonna get through all this
junk?
Debby, the other shredder. This one just died. And no calls,
                puleeze!
        Dring! Dring!
Debby, I said, no calls! It's your wife, sir.
My wife only calls to my cell. But she said, . . . Okay,
put her on then. Huh? No miss, I haven't found your poems.
                Hangs up.
        Dammit!
Why am I doing this? This is a dog's life, really!
Here's more silly stuff . . . on dogs! Figures. Shreds it. On poetry.
Shreds it. On sex. Shreds it. Great prose perhaps, but poetry?
                My foot!
        Jesus!
Fifty pages long! You *really* think I'm gonna
read them all? Did you read the guidelines? Now this: too maudlin.
And this: gibberish, nothing else. This free verse isn't any better.
                Shreds it.
        How cute:
quoting famous lines ad infinitum, another fad.
Look at this: Because I could not stop for death, blah-blah; and
miles to go before I sleep, blah-blah. Well, *I* could use a good nap.
                Shreds it.
        Now this:
your typical poetry workshop stuff. In pidgin English,
oh boy. Shreds it. If *this* is the state of affairs in poetry, good Lord!
Hey, do any of you poets know what I am going through here
every day?
                Do you?
        What now?
My name? In the *title*? It better be good.
Who *is* this guy? Freddy. Freddy Newbie? Hm, anyway,
let's give it a read. It's just one page; no, two—
                all right.
        Hm, but
this is great! Wow, it's the damndest

112

truth he's writing about, and truth is beauty,
like good old Keats said, and beauty is truth. Heck, it's really
                              awesome!
        I bet
I could have written it myself. It's all about *me!*
Finally someone out there who understands my plight. I've got to
publish this, backlog or not. Deb, I'm gone for a week. Shred the
rest
                    of the month.

THE FREIGHT TRAIN FROM HOUSTON

When I drive every morning at 8 a.m.
to the railroad crossing here at Route number 10,
I'm always late, and must wait, wait, wait
because the crossing gate just went down.
Then there is that distant bang,
soon becoming a definite clang
of metal on metal . . . Is *that* all?
No, no! It isn't, for here comes the engine —
the SOLID, COLOSSAL E N G I N E —
and there's the Steel and Squeal
of Clattering, Rattling, Dazzling Wheels
of freight cars jerking, shaking and grinding, for
HERE — COMES — THUNDERING — PAST —
WITH RACKET, RUMBLE, SMOKE, AND BLAST:
T H E   F R E I G H T   T R A I N,
      the Northbound Freight Train From Houston, Texas!

The longest freight I've ever seen around;
the loudest too with ear-splitting sounds.
Horns screeching and screaming —
wheels grumbling and steaming —
earth rocking and shaking like hell.
Cars growling and thumping —
rails groaning and jumping —
the clanging air BLARES with the BELL.
      Is this an earthquake?
      No, no! This is the freight train from Houston,
      tearing apart a sleepy morning in Jackson,
      hurrying past at breakneck speed—
      SPEED — SPEED — SPEED — BREAKNECK SPEED
WHOOSH — WHOOSH — away to the north!

When oh when can we cross the railroad track
to forge ahead and never come back.
How long is the train coming round the bend
while we wait, wait, wait for the end.
Here comes a freight car with carrots and peas.
Here comes another with butter and cheese.
      Tons of boxes with juicy tomatoes
      on top of beef and sweet potatoes.
FOOOOOOOD—FOOOOOOOD—and FREIGHT,
racing and chasing through the state!
      But here comes the smoke that sickens,
      choking the artichokes and chicken:
      thick, black smoke sweeping everywhere,
      making us cough while gasping for air.
The Din Is Deafening. This Is BEDLAM.
A Hundred Freight Cars, MAD With Rhythm!
      Is this an earthquake?
      No, no! This is the freight train from Houston,
      acing and chasing with FREIGHT—FOOD—FREIGHT—
      wrecking and shaking the STATE—TOOT—WAIT!—
thundering on to the north!

Oh, how I long for the sound of
nothing . . . nothing . . . nothing . . .
but the wheels on the gaps in the rails repeat:
Clickeding . . . clickeding . . . clickeding . . .
Oh, how I long for the opposite side,
where all is lovely, quiet and wide . . .
quiet and wide . . . quiet . . . quiet . . .

But what is this sudden break in the din?
Is there then an end to all that thunder?
Clickeding-ding . . . clickeding . . . ding . . .
ching . . . ding . . . ching-a-ding . . . ching . . . ching

Oh, yes, now this is all different:
nothing . . . nothing . . . nothing . . .
The tail of the train has finally past,
and here's the empty track at last.
Colossal loads are moving forth.
Wheels are slowly fading somewhere north . . .
     Was there an earthquake?
     Was there a freight train?
Nothing . . . nothing . . . nothing . . .
I'm crossing the railroad track,
and God will know when I'll come back.
Quiet and wide . . . quiet . . . quiet . . .
Twitter, tweet . . . twitter, twitter . . . tweet, tweet

STRANGE RENEWAL

A book falls open on a random page:
a dream labyrinth of footsteps,
echoing times I never knew.
 A love, forgotten;
 tears, vanished.
 A limber gait, that's all.

A dream reality is moving ahead of me.
Will I follow? When?
Tracks, unseen from where I was or
 where I'm going.
 Newer pages. Many—
 blank, unwritten.

Returning from a different past. Did I know?
Didn't I? Answers recede. A tale continues:
I'm in it — no, not me.
 Where I was is where it's going.
 Who's pushing me ahead
 and back, over and over?

Outside, all is the same, and yet not quite.
Inside, strange renewal: a house, windows,
a door — chasms in time,
 overwhelming. A high sky
 and far shadow, waiting.
 The book closes by itself . . .

THE CHIMES OF THE CLOCK AT THE COURTHOUSE

I miss the chimes of the clock at the Courthouse,
their steady, soulful clang at the top of the hour,
so dependable, as if to tell us: Yes, I'm still here.

They used to wake me up every morning at seven:
clang!...clang!...clang! Seven times all across the city,
unmistakably present, sonorous and clear.

Dang! I haven't heard them ring out in weeks!
I'm gonna give the Courthouse a ring to fix things.
This dead silence feels void and hollow to my ears.

I miss those deep, solemn chimes of the clock at the
Courthouse and wonder how many of us also crave
their soothing *clang!...clang!...clang!* So calm, so dear...

IN SCULPTED SENTENCES OF VERBOSE PROSE

Or the Impasse in Poetry in Fifteen Wordy but Telling Stanzas

In sculpted sentences of verbose prose,
the sculptor of modern poems chisels
his ideas in structures of clever language,
touching the inner world of the Muse
almost never . . .

Rarely caring for overall balance, or
clear concepts of form, he wildly hacks
away at both, tearing down tried-and-true
building blocks of art with strained verbiage
of minimal content.

He mistrusts poetic vision and even
license, but rather favors novel abstractions,
as if potent, human sentiments were
too mundane for words, or worse: *poems*
you can *feel* for once.

His endless soliloquies aimlessly
drag, reminding us of what is most
forgettable. How many of his titles
will be remembered for more than
say . . . two minutes?

He finds, and God knows why, that to
sound contrived, abstruse or learned
more than others is *the thing* to do,
missing out on having fun with the
Muse for a change.

See how he skilfully rejects emotion,
or, to please his peers and metaphors,
cuts off clarity, too, making sure
that real obscurity shows in all of his
stillborn imagery.

Having little of an individual voice,
other than his own misguided ego, does
wonders in the poetic landscape of his
era where a classic Muse is considered
too old hat.

Will he ever contemplate throwing
something passionate into the mix,
in stead of absence of substance he's
coming up with, presenting *that* as
ho hum, deep?

He may get truly inspired, but his love
for complexities doesn't help, and thus
he excels in making many of us nod off
in seconds. *Everyone* knows it now,
but when will *he?*

But see, he hardly revels in revelatory
rhythms, nor does he re-create or mold
a form of art that knows a future, so it
comes as no surprise he *will* mistake
prose for poems.

Using his favorite tool: amorphousness,
he manages making what could be
meaningful meaningless, donning Her some
catchy title to appease Her, but She
is not amused.

No matter how he frantically hunts
for up-to-date subject matter, the
Muse doesn't need such flattery. After
all, She *has* a famous name, a form and
mystery already.

She yawns because adventure never
enters here. None of his sprawling sentences
make Her magic soar in language
hard as nails where words, ideas and poets
simply choke.

His creativity struggles with an
art form he doesn't really serve. He's
yet to find a way to recognize the
far horizons She inhabits, which She
transcends alone.

Trapped between shaky intent and doubtful
outcome, the sculptor sits, staring at the
Muse getting ready now to leave forever,
stripped of what *he* thought would be the
purest Poetry . . .

WILD GEESE FROM CANADA

There's big cackling in the night.
The geese have left their nests in Canada
And pass our home en route to Florida.
I trust they'll find their goal all right.

Nature leads them where to go.
They formed a gaggling band, and off they went,
And now they fade and think they all will spend
A winter minus all that snow.

Autumn has been making giant strides—
We've seen such early signs before. The cold
Will follow pretty soon, and snow will bolt
Each little home on every side.

Now, we're happy here and share,
And if we can't remove the snow alone,
We'll still be fine, for there's enough at home
To feed us while we loaf and care.

But if winter storms would cause us harm,
We *could* decide to spread our arms and try
To join those *geese* and leave to Nature why
She wants us where it's snug and warm . . .

Something really weird is in the air—
I'm getting lighter, almost like a feather . . .
Is something pulling me to better weather?
Let's ask our feathered friends up there.

Here's the window, there the sky—
We're taking off together, wing to wing.
We're flying down to Florida, to spring.
Bye, bye now, Iowa, goodbye.

To Florida, Florida! But what was *that?*
(I heard a chuckle coming from your mouth.)
You're *cackling* while we're flapping south!
(Oh are you nudging me, or what?)

(There *was* a tapping by my shoulder)—
We're catching up now with our flock and kin
And should be hitting Florida by nine a.m.
(Strange enough it's getting colder).

But hey, all is well that ends well:
We're quickly heading down now for the landing,
Flapping closely just like geese of standing,
(But *you* are wiggling here like *hell*).

(Oh you're just tossing and turning tonight)—
We've been in bed to dream of warmer Florida
Like gaggles flying by from good old Canada.
(We're staying home to snuggle up all right).

BOOKS

Sometimes, when I think of the vast wisdom ever
contained in books; countless scriptures of all creeds;

scrolls in indecipherable languages; tomes of science;
the great Library of Alexandria destroyed by fire

centuries ago, priceless knowledge gone; thousands
of books burned by the Third Reich; books still held

secret at the Vatican; hieroglyphs in Egypt and
whatever Atlantis may have contributed to the written

word; books simply lost and never found; others
molded, fallen apart, discarded, and all the many

books I'll never be able to read in a lifetime, even if
I lived a thousand years; and when I think of all these

while browsing at garage sales, used bookstores (oh,
the good feel of an old book and the sense of care for

books you surmise some previous owner had; to see
his or her name written on the title page, sometimes

with the date of purchase or gift — yes, then I tend
to hold a book in my hands a little long sometimes,

deliberating whether I'll buy, and I read again what's
on the flap; scan a few more pages; look for a keen

phrase here and there; ponder on the title, the design,
the author's name, weighing it all in my hand . . . and

page after page of long-forgotten lore, adventure and
myth slowly take shape, mingling with my own memory

of myth in the back of my mind, passing through my
skin, stealing into my bones, my heart; holding me

spellbound for a lifetime it seems, and somehow
beneath my feet the deeper caves and mysteries of

the earth open wide where I can glimpse that which I
cannot name but know that it exists; and I'm feeling

strangely rooted and connected to all cultures, beliefs,
poetry, wars, romance, history, peace, and then I *may*

take the book home, but as I'm standing here, lost in
time for a while, *some* power is reclaiming everything

I thought was lost to Man one time, and I see the
Great Communicator of it all in all these many chapters,

paragraphs, sentences, words, working their way with
a purpose, meaning, and conviction across so many

ages, and suddenly it seems that everything is here
now, and really never went away at all as long as books

have ever existed and readers found them, and as I
close the book, walking out to get some fresh air,

there's all the magic in the air as of old still . . .
and I can live with that and be an open book to all.

THE NEW YORK CITY ZOO

Tell me, have you ever been to New York City?
Have you seen the rat race there and kept your wits?

I have sailed the roughest seas and crossed the deserts—
I have fought ferocious tigers in Bengal—
Dangers of the Congo jungles do not scare me—
I have climbed the steepest mountains in Nepal—
I have known the perils of Caracas, Rio, Shanghai, Cairo,
Yet they're trifles when compared to New York City's.

Hell, there's nothing quite like New York City.
Let me tell you, it's a scary, noisy jungle.
    There is nothing, nothing like it.
        It's insane. It's a racket.
        Most unnerving
    And chaotic.
It's a zoo.
It's a jungle, and a total, total zoo!

Tell me, have you ever passed through New York City?
Have you braved the traffic jams and lived to tell?

Take your chances when you cross Manhattan.
You'll be lucky if you never lose your cool.
Savage tiger taxis leap through intersections.
Buses scoot like angry rhinos by the curb.
Motorized gorillas roar around the plazas.
Twenty million legs and roaches hit the town.

    How they hurry, hurry, always hurry.
    From one crowded corner to the next.
    Busy, busy, busy, always busy.
    Dammit, can they never once relax?

See, there's nothing quite like New York City.
It's like rush hours always in this noisy, nutty den.
    There is nothing, nothing you can

Do about it.
Oh forget it.
It's a madhouse.
It's a jungle. No, it's
Intenser than a jungle, zoo, or racket.

So you want to come and live in New York City—
Have you lost your marbles somewhere on the way?

Take the smelly subway if you really dare.
Hyenas, snakes, and panthers track you there.
Ambulances, cops, and bears compete on Second.
Cheetahs sneak behind you, snooping for your dough.
Hordes of hasty penguins stalk the zebra crossings.
Wildebeests and sharks attack the crazy crowd.

How they rush you, rush you, always rush you,
Racing down the overcrowded streets.
Faster, faster, faster, always faster—
Faster than Arabian mares in heat.

Are you sure you want to work in New York City?
Do you dream of bigger bucks and Wall Street stocks?

Sure, we have the Empire State, fantastic Building.
When you gaze below, you wouldn't ever think
That New York City was a jungle, den, or zoo.
Yes, we have the Esplanade at Brooklyn Heights.
When you watch the skyline rise across the river,
Truly, New York City is a shining dream...

But you cannot dream that dream forever.
You *must* come down and cross the stream.
Soon you act New Yorkian and you hurry,
And so you lose your peaceful, Sunday dream.

Every day more hopefuls want to join this place.
Are you crazy? What's your hurry? There's no space.
And yet, there's something special here in New York City,
Even though this town is way too hectic for my nerves.

So here is how
    I handle all of that these days.
    Oh I love it,
  'Cause it's so endearing
Since I simply lounge and work now at
My refuge at the good old New York City Zoo.

I will confess there was a time I was a nervous wreck,
But see, somehow I went through hell and made it back.
To keep me sane, I used to cruise the New York City Zoo.
I had to cross Manhattan somehow daily, *and* I made it, too.

    You see, my lions here are all so peaceful...
    Well sure, they roar like in the jungle,
    And yet... they won't attack you.
    All my wolves and jaguars look so docile...
    And if they growl, it's in their nature,
    But no... they won't harass you.

    My birds sing gorgeous tunes all day.
    Flamingos bow with grace and bend a leg.
    My placid camels nibble at a bale of hay.
    Gazelles approach the fence and sweetly beg.

But to get there safely, I'd be crossing wild Manhattan, too.
So *I* would run from *zoo* to Zoo, and back from Zoo to *zoo*.
I swear to God that no one can escape
The New York City vultures, bats, and apes.
They chase your ass around the block
All day all night around the clock.

No, there's nothing quite like New York City,
But what I've found here is so precious
    In the Zoo in New York City,
        'Cause I get to daily
        Feed the cutest
    Leopards at the
New York City Zoo.
That's my job now. I'm so happy. *They* are happy, too.

Here I can forget the hustle and bustle
Of all that restless, New York City life.
Believe me, at the Zoo there is no hassle.
Now I lead a much more quiet life.

Please come visit at my darling Zoo.
I'll let you pet my talking cockatoo.
My monkeys surely will endear you.
I've trained them so they'll pet you, too.
All the species are so peaceful at my Zoo,
In my haven at the New York City Zoo.

How they love you, love you, always love you,
Often moving me to tears.
Yes, they simply love you, always love you,
Making you forget your fears.

See? There's nothing quite like New York City.
Now, before you pack your stuff and move
To New York City,
Tell me, is it *you*,
Or the jungle,
Or the racket,
Or the zoo in *you* that's calling *you* to the City?

Well, if you come to live in New York City,
All of us will love you, always love you,
'Cause we're all like humans and should love you—
Here in the Zoo, and out in the City.

Apples and Oranges

A Play on Words and Concepts in Five Short Acts

1

In good old mathematics,
cubes and spheres appear
as flawless, divine creations.

2

But please don't compare them,
or they quickly morph into
merely apples and oranges.

3

As spherical creations,
apples and oranges look
almost like neat spheres.

4

In mathematics, cubes and
spheres assume their given part
assigned by science.

5

But apples and oranges grow
on two of God's fine trees whose
creations swell for us to eat!

YOUR FACE

Oh, where was there on earth
A face so kind?
Somewhere in dreams perhaps,
Deep in my mind?
How would it shine, but far
Like stars will do.
I've wished it in my sphere,
And with it: *you*.

I've reached for it to bask
Within its gleam
And hold it close to me
Like in some dream.
It's like the radiant star
I've longed to find:
The spark, the smiling glance
Where love is kind.

Oh, why then was I born
To misunderstand
Some distant star looking once
Like promised land?
Is love then only a dream
Of a face above?
Is love then only a sigh
For deeper love?

I thought that I could touch
A face like that.
I should have known that love
Is more than that—
And though we may have seemed
So close above,
There is a pause . . . On *earth*
I've lost that love.

And now it's over since
I've touched that star.
I've loved a dream, and now
You're fading far,
But *why* was there on earth
A face so dear?
For dreams of stars perhaps,
Deep in a tear . . . ?

HEALING

A cut this deep can
keep an unstitched
wound apart for days.
Can it be healed?
It just depends...

The hurt our hearts
have felt goes deep,
but let's not part...
Let's meet to heal
it now as friends!

SMALL TOWN ROUTINE - ONE VIEW

Routine . . . routine . . . routine . . .
Nothing . . . no traffic at all, not even a dog.
Just the house across the street staring back.

But what was that? . . . A break in the routine?
Something happening down the street, right?
Stillness . . . nothing important it seems . . .

I look out my narrow window again:
Then, a cyclist I know *by name* pedals by
from left to right to the grocery store.

Once more . . . nothing . . . stillness . . .
I've lived here way too long.
But *have* I lived?

SMALL TOWN ROUTINE - A DIFFERENT VIEW

Routine . . . routine . . . and more routine . . .
Well, here's a break in the routine for you!

Something just happened down the street, right?
I look out through the narrow window . . .

Nothing . . . no traffic at all, not even a stray cat—
just the building across the street staring back . . .

Dead quiet . . . nothing important it seems . . . *ah, but now:*
a bicyclist I know *by name* flits by from left to right! Gone.

Once more . . . dead quiet . . . so total . . .
Small town indeed, but *WHAT an exciting day!*

THE ADDRESSEE

The day I become able to address this old, old
hurt, it will be like dispatching and promptly
receiving a letter back destined to arrive at a
better place inside my self where its contents
must have been known long before the old, old
shame was revealed, and there's only one line:
Dear friend, it's all gone now, and for good.

TROPICAL JUNGLE IN THE AMAZON

A Lyrical-Dramatic Tableau in Two Semi-Identical Parts

INNOCENCE

Mysteriously beautiful . . .
Morning sunlight streaming in
On gleaming, opulent green . . .
Darker flora at one side of a
Tall, magnificent mahogany tree . . .

Thick drops of dew on graceful fern twigs
Grandly bowing down . . .
Yellow bill toucans screaming at one another high in trees.
A timid, red hibiscus flower opening up beneath . . .

A sudden thump on the forest floor! Another one!!
A dead branch falling . . . ?
Coconuts dropping . . . ?

The nameless presence of lurking, unknown gods
Peering out of more than a thousand eyes.
Heavy silence . . . The onset of tangible heat . . .
A loose liana hanging down, motionless . . .
The morning call of monkeys, almost musical . . .
Singing of birds, magical . . .

An abrupt rustle in the underbrush!!!
Creaking, dead wood as if surreptitiously being stepped on . . .
A hungry beast of prey . . . ?
A creepy croc or anaconda . . . ?
A pack of Cocoma cannibals . . . ?
A silence of ages . . .
My imagination . . . ? Who knows . . . ?

FEAR

Dangerously beautiful . . .
Deep poisonous green and patches of lurid light
Obliquely streaking past a hidden, horrid pair of eyes . . .
An immense shadow by the side of a mahogany tree!
The distinct presence of dark, perhaps deadly entities . . .
Stifling silence . . . Heat . . . Crushing heat . . . Inconceivable
    heat . . .

A flesh—eating flower, blood red . . .
A violent stir in the undergrowth!!!
A panther on the prowl . . . ?
A boa looking for lunch . . . ?
Or some other man—eating animal . . . ?
Or some very hungry *cannibals?!?!?!?!?*
About to feast after fasting for eleven days and a half?
Aaaahhh, what's that stab in the middle of my back?
An arrow dipped in poison?
Or just a fatal heart attack?
A twitching nerve along my spinal marrow?

A liana sweeping in circles before me!
Bloodcurdling cries all around me!!
Cannibalistic laughter and
DRUMS! DRUMS!! DRUMS!!! Tremendous DRUMS!!!!
Apelike shrieks and
EYES! EYES!! EYES!!! Everywhere EYES!!!!
Ten Thousand Eyes!!!!!!!!!!!—

Five thousand cannibals???? What kind of cannibals?
Cocomas who roast you live with clothes on?
Tucanos who boil your heart and entrails?
Tapuyas who chop you up and swallow you raw?
Are they gonna suck up my blood with a straw?
Why on earth did I get so big and fat?
Why did mom always feed me like that?
Couldn't I leave all those calories alone?
Will *hungry* cannibals leave *me* alone?

Noooooooooooooooooooooooooo!
Aren't they coming down now in endless rows?
Ooooooooooooooooooooooooo!
Are they . . . ? But . . . where . . . are . . . they . . . ?

A silence of *ten thousand ages* . . . No cannibals . . . ?
A sudden bang on the forest floor, quite close!!!
And another one—and another . . .

Coconuts . . . ?
    Cannibals . . . ?
        My imagination . . . ?
            Who knows . . . ?

A NEW DAWN

ETERNAL SOURCE

1

bubble up, eternal source —
follow your recurring course — slither down from mountain
slopes —
gather into rivulets — sweep the valleys — pass the hills.

make a turn and broaden here —
overflow with cataracts — fill the rivers — form the lakes —
mirror all the sky and swell, and flow into the ocean.

bubble up — evaporate —
disappear into the air — make tornados, thunderheads —
sail away on tumbling winds — float and rest among the clouds . . .

2

turn around and look below —
pour if you are inclined to — hit the ocean — beat the land —
leap the breakers — lap the shore — stretch across the open sea.

and now enjoy your being
like the ocean does all day — roll and play and live and dream —
heave with billows to the main, and reach to each horizon.

rise and fall with tidal waves —
spin below in vortices — mix with hidden undercurrents —
touch the silent ocean floor — join the essence of it all . . .

3

roll on, ocean — find the coast —
do not tarry in the gulf — meet the rivers — leave the bay —
cross the pools, lagoons and lakes — revel with the waterfalls.

bubble up and undulate —
spread the message of the deep — enter grottos, clefts and pores —
connect to water everywhere — soak the thirsty, waiting soil . . .

hear the trickle of the spring —
ripple over creek and rill — run with rapids down the stream —
let no stagnant water be — follow your recurring course —

bubble up, eternal source.

THE DOE

*The thirst of the soul is sweeter than the wine
of material things, and the fear of the spirit is
dearer than the security of the body.*
—Kahlil Gibran

Why so afraid to bow down,
My dear one, my daughter?
Doesn't the doe go daily down to her spring?
Doesn't the spring, brimming with water,
Flow like a river, down to the sea?

Why so afraid to look up,
My dear one, my daughter?
Doesn't the sea always look at the sky?
Doesn't the cloud, cherishing water,
Rain in cycles back to the sea?

You are thirsty for spirit,
My dear little doe.
You're alone, thirsty, and yet you resemble
A cool oasis brimming with water
Where birds gather and sing.

I am trusting. You know it,
My dear little doe.
Be your journey as trustful, for I'll be going;
Like rivers receding, their waters
Flowing back to their spring.

Don't be afraid to look up,
My daughter, my dear one.
Haven't my hands dried all of your tears?
You'll be my doe, my daughter,
No matter where I may go.

Don't be afraid to bow down,
My daughter, my dear one.
Heaven still spans all over your tears.
Won't you come down to the water
Now and drink, dear little doe?

AWESTRUCK AT NIAGARA FALLS

The shattering din and ever-louder roar
on approaching the waterfall,
ear-splitting almost to the max—
the steep drop of mega zillions of gallons
of crashing, growling water,
and the sheer, awe-inspiring wonder
the first time I saw
the turbulent magnitude
of Niagara Falls
had my little boy asking me that day, "Daddy,
what's a waterfall?"
As I was thinking hard what to
tell him about my mounting impressions
of that massive outpouring of water
and the deafening, hypnotic power
of it all, almost pulling you clear over the edge,
he showed me in his own simple way, as we got closer,
what Niagara Falls
meant to him by his wide-eyed face at seeing
how much water was coming down;
and how he covered his ears—his tiny
silhouette etched against that huge backdrop
of roaring water,
aghast at the sly and enticing lure
of the beckoning abyss;
and how he ran into daddy's big arms to safely
watch Niagara Falls!

Awestruck and thunderstruck, but fiercely together—
my son holding on to me for dear life and I to him—
we watched the overwhelming, shatter-splattering,
water-whelming walls upon walls upon walls
of clattering, clash-blasting, raging tons and tons
of water never-ending,
bowling us over, almost hurling us downward into
the Savage, Merciless, Rock-Splitting,
ROARING, DRONING,

WRECKING, THUNDERING,
ROAR—RUMBLING M A E L S T R O M of
T—O—T—A—L   P—A—N—D—E—M—O—N—I—U—M—
mounting to huge, primordial, clang—towering soundscapes
of blangering, rattling, thundering bragh and droning brang;
obliterating every sense of self I've ever known
with cataclysmic, heart stopping vistas of clashing clangor—
ever-louder—
loud beyond comparison or conception even;
rending any lurking memory of quietude to shreds,
and any reasonable thought to a jumble of meaningless nothings—
impossible to describe in words
as words get completely ripped apart, chopped off,
bent out of shape to become unrecognizable,
lose their meaning,
thunderously disappearing, reappearing,
but differently,
resembling nothing, not even sound,
roaring away again without trace
back into the crashing, crazy chaos of noise
blasting downward at Niagara Falls!
How could I ever tell my son what a real waterfall is,
as everything I ever thought it was, was being made ridiculous
by this untamed power
bursting wide open with just all-out sound,
undifferentiated, primal, tribal, and intense;
approaching madness almost;
simultaneously incomprehensible and making some sort of sense,
yet totally unfathomably so;
washing over everything;
drowning out and eroding everything in its path;
and shatter-shaking the very rock under Niagara Falls.
In the midst of all that infernal cacophony
where you cannot hear your own voice,
even if you screamed your lungs out for help,
my son pointed on high to the
many, many rainbows arching over the bubbling spray clouds
to where the old Niagara River must have decided once
to go over the edge and start falling down,
down, down, forevermore down,

146

to fall, fall, and fall,
and then fell, fell, and fell;
kept falling, tumbling, rumbling, thundering;
is still falling, crashing and droning;
falls, falls and falls; ceaselessly falls
crash-shattering into the seething, thundering,
awesome cauldron
of Niagara Falls;
and then to proceed, gradually becalming,
becoming a river all over again, past the clamor,
past the thunder where once it fell,
flowing toward a quieter space far away
to where we all are headed,
far beyond anything like Niagara Falls
faintly echoing, still echoing
in the back of my mind
as I am driving now my boy back home . . .

A New Dawn

There's a lovely icicle
tapering straight down
from a rooftop in January,

as if doomed
to point forever downward
like stubborn stalactites—

dreamlike . . . frozen . . .
fiercely glistening against an icy dawn,
yet happy to be hanging in there,

but also resigned to someday
melt, trickle down and
morph into one shiny puddle

looking up high to finally,
boldly mirror a new dawn,
glimpsed by early passersby

dreaming one lucid moment
of better tomorrows,
maybe in March . . .

SHELL SONG

After a swim
I stepped ashore
and found a shell
by Bari, Italy.
I held it to
my ear to hear
the ocean sing,
and yes, there was
a pretty tune,
for now a boy
of maybe four
walked by, singing.

Halfway in the
song he turned to
ask me *who*
I was—how *old*
I was—*where* I
came from—and
where *that* was.
In poor Italian
I replied, "There,
across the sea."
"What is *that* in
English then?"
I turned around—
He meant the sea.

"The sea," I said.
"And this, and that?"
"The shore, the sky."
"And where do they
live?" he asked.
I shrugged—puzzled.
"And what is *this*?"
He grabbed my shell
and put it to

his ear and smiled,
but when I failed to
answer, he got up.
I hurried then to
say, "A shell," but
that he never heard
I think because
he walked away,
singing his ditty.

Too soon his smallish
voice faded away.
I watched the surf
along the shore,
and then the sound
of silence came . . .
and then again
the sound of waves.
I tossed my shell
into the sea,
and there it sank
by Bari, Italy.

And there it lies
with other shells,
until the tide
returns them, *if*
at all. If one
could tell me why
the sea, the shore,
the sky are what
they are, then I'd
be young again
to play all day
like little boys
on sunny shores.
If I live to hear
that song again
beside the
breakers' roar,

I will return to
pick a shell and
listen to the boy who
told me who I was,
and I will hum
inside my shell,
and join the sea.

A Reluctant, Little Ode to Snow

Oh no, too much snow!
You fickle miracle of nature,
altering all,
idly flitting to furtively fall . . .

You spring from naught,
oh aerial messenger of candor,
swirling away,
slowly changing a darker day.

Oh snow, and then
becoming part of every structure,
snowing on snow,
softly shushing the snow below.

Shucks! That's how we get
your sleet and slush to ponder on,
slipping, sliding, and
cursing one more damn winter!

It's been so awfully nice
to suffer your ice-cold blizzards
making us run for
cover, yearning for summer.

You come and go,
a fitful panorama of winter,
melting away,
leaving no trace of white today.

But then again, tonight
you conjured up a makeover
of snow all over,
somehow making

the enigma and
tender wonder of winter
memorable now,
revealing new meaning in snow.

Y'know, that hokey
'Winter Wonderland' misnomer
for once entirely
fitted — but oh so briefly . . .

OCEAN SONG

To be read in an even manner

I

I am unending, gentle motion
I am the ocean
I reach each continent on earth
I view them all with mirth
I meet the rivers
I am the giver
I escort ships from every side
And rock them lightly on the tide
I guide them with my hand
And safely lead them to the land

II

I am incredibly in motion
I am the ocean
I push huge waves wherever I can
To smash the world of Man
I send my breakers
I am the taker
I kick all ships and chase them on
And will not rest until they're gone
I seize them with my claws
To grandly fling them to my jaws

III

I am no longer in motion
I am the ocean
I am serene from east to west
And all myself at rest
I've found devotion
I am the ocean

I am a mirror of God's own light
Reflecting His love each day each night
I am the open sea
And continents incline to me

IV

I've crossed the billows of emotion
I am the ocean
I left them back along the way
I've seen they were mere foam and spray
I've joined the placid Gulf Stream
Some force engulfed them
My fingers span the globe with ease
I have become the Seven Seas
I flow to you my land
I dream a sparkling gem upon my hand

V

I am the all unfolding motion
I am the ocean
I am all yours with all my heart
In you I'm taking part
I am emerging
There's no more searching
I am your one returning friend
I've come to you embracing land
I've found you in my arms
You're here forever safe and warm

VI

I am eternally in motion
I am the ocean
And so I travel round the world
On lofty waves unfurled

I roll forever
I leave you never
I am the soul within your reach
I stretch with you upon your beach
I am your dream come true
It breathes and moves and lives in you

VII

It is the heart and soul of motion
It is the ocean
It is in motion at your will
It heaves and yet it's still
It is devotion
It's like an ocean
It's for the ocean and for Man
To crown it where it all began
I'm opening up my hand
And there's the sea and here the land

ALMOST SUMMER

*Happiness is the absence
of the striving for happiness.*
—Chuang-tzu

This is one of those days
you lie down on the soft grass
    and pick a flower,
    twirling it for hours,
thinking of nothing, nothing at all.

Ants discover your hand—
and you? Well, you don't mind,
    besides, it feels kinda nice.
    You think you're getting wise,
while far away the clouds stately sail.

A mild sun is about,
and nothing you ever have known
    will spoil this weather.
    Your mind is almost in summer,
floating on slow waves lightly away.

You're alone, and nobody else
but you is dreaming away the day.
    You're gazing on high,
    wondering just why now the sky
is all that you care for today.

Three, four birds are warbling
lovely tweets from a tree,
    secretly capturing
    all of your being. Enraptured
you listen before they quietly leave.

Ah, you're almost lost now
while silence on silence descends.
    You're not at all here.
    Nothing on earth interferes.
A deepest of blue is all you're seeing.

Your day is like a ray
from a land where summers arise.
		The sun is touching you freely,
		and this is what you're feeling:
your life is as bright as your being.

The light and the shadows
are having the time of their lives:
		From numerous branches outspread,
		a tree overhead
sheds patterns, rich in shade and repose.

You feel you could stay there
like clouds suspended above.
		It doesn't surprise you
		that the horizon,
though distant, seems tangibly close.

You can't for a moment
imagine that this day will end.
		There's nothing quite like it:
		All is so perfect,
and haven't you always known why that is so?

The grass is so mellow—
All of a sudden a breeze
		blows all through your hair.
		You're *at one* with the air,
but why are you stretching? Planning to go?

Mmmmm???
This awesome summer day?
		I don't think so,
		No,
not today . . .

Flying to Miami

America is under me.
We have been flying high.
The clouds nearby extend
like snowy down across the lovely blue.

The years I do not like to count
are slowly passing by.
The space beyond my porthole is my friend,
and I can watch the sky for miles and miles.

I've left my state; I'm stateless now—
I rest and glide on air.
For all I know I'm pretty safe on high.
I think I'll be okay.

Miami is my stop for now,
and then? Who knows? I guess
I need some sun again.
I long to rest and crave a warmer state.

Has Florida not always been
a precious dream
I prized no matter what?
The trees there used to sway so gracefully.

As I recall, the passion flower
often was abloom—
the fragrant breeze
a soothing wave from paradise.

I almost feel my body lying there,
and even sense,
beneath my naked back,
a golden beach now stretching far for miles—

but here I am, flying to that place of
sun tan, beaches, dollars and hotels
while this America is under me and waits.
I still can change my life.

PINE NEEDLE

Metamorphosis

I'm looking down at a
far, secret valley of trees.
Tall stands of pine fade
towards the horizon.

Something keeps telling me
I'm about to float
and skim along the slope
to join a slow breeze.

As I'm watching a stir
in that giant surface
of clustering treetops
patterned like a brush,

I'm starting to feel
like one of those pines,
their needles waving
grandly in the wind

swaying my tree now
with one, huge hush . . .
and suddenly I am
being severed, gliding

over deep forests
holding no secrets at all.
Those who still dream
on the hill may not get this:

Here, everything is solved,
and each tree stands still.
Pine needles won't fall.
I soar above a magic land.

Spring Is Like a Young, Wonderful Woman

Spring is like a young, wonderful woman.
When *she* comes round, I am a man.
Just look at those soft, shapely hills.
   I can gaze at them for hours,
     And she'll wave back from each new flower,
       But, I must wait.

Always is the air full of her fragrance
As if she just flew by on wings.
From a sunbeam she will step down
   And tap me on the shoulder,
     Making me feel I'll never grow older,
       And that is totally great.

I'm absolutely certain she isn't
Just some poet's fancy on the fly.
The fresh, young green is her domain,
   And it is her lovely custom
     To each morning hang a fuller blossom
       Around the trees.

Her voice is ringing with the morning thrushes
While I am listening behind a bush.
I cannot see her—she's so quick.
   I often find myself musing:
     What would my life be without her moving
       High with each breeze.

Warm qualities abound in her nature,
And all day long she'll cast them here.
Incredibly bright is her smile
   And wider than each horizon.
     Loudly she will laugh, shaking the heavens,
       Making them rain.

Cooler qualities arise in her also,
But not for long. The rain will go,
And soon she'll descend from the clouds,
    Scattering her freshest blessings,
    Meanwhile vibrantly taking possession
        Of earth again.

And so she dances through her season,
And everywhere I follow her signs.
Sometimes, on quiet afternoons,
    I'd swear I was getting closer—
    Yes, I know I'm afraid to lose her.
        She knows that, too.

She may withdraw by night into darkness
Where stars remind me of her eyes,
But then she rises with the moon.
    Her hair on the night wind streaming
    Gives ample opportunity for dreaming
        Of what I'd like to do.

There'll come a day when she'll be summer
To tease me yet another year.
She is eternal and *I* am human.
    Perhaps she is the goddess of nature.
    Perhaps I was some god once who loved her
        When we were young.

Yet if she stops being that one woman,
I'll wait for her with all mankind.
She's dear to me like beauty's bloom.
    Someday, I shan't be around her,
    But *she* will linger where you'll find her
        In song after song.

THE QUIET WAY OF UNFORGOTTEN TREES

The trees along the way
once cast a most delightful shade,
but that's so many years ago.

They're gone forever now,
but still I think their image will not fade.
We always prized those days.

The sun would shimmer on their crowns—
A breeze would sway their branches there—
so grand their tall, receding rows...

The way is very quiet now
and full of much too open space...where
once so many birds had flown.

GIANT SEQUOIA

A Hymn

I

O *Sequoiadendron giganteum,*
Oldest and grandest of beings,
Noblest of souls in the world,
You've long been present in my timeless thoughts,
And I am hearing your higher silence waving over all.

II

Heaven seems to be your foremost ideal —
For ages have I seen you grow,
Largest of trees in the world.
A tiny seed contained your kingly race,
And deep in my heart I feel your countless roots, deep in my breast.

III

Is there anywhere anyone like you?
Prior to Buddha and Christ,
Your grandeur graced the world,
And since you've entered the plane of the greats,
Your lofty span has linked the times of old to those of today.

IV

Generations have lived, passed, and returned.
Who hasn't admired your crown?
From your crest you view the world.
Straight and proud, but oh, so tender are you,
My *Sequoiadendron giganteum,* beloved being.

165

V

Forests like yours are grand cathedrals —
Quietness among your groves is whole.
Born within that pristine world
Where sunbeams break through mist and early dawn,
Your day is an age in bright surroundings. Your nights are light.

VI

On the slopes of the Sierra Nevada
Gather and rise my sequoias.
Their being in my world
Is one of more than peace and harmony.
With outstretched arms and lifted face, they live and live and live!

VII

Fires nor floods nor storms subdue them.
They clutch the earth and touch the sky,
Strongest of trees in the world!
Though man tried hard once to destroy their kind,
They won't be conquered—where they dwell, they share their
domain.

VIII

As gigantic as their presence is,
So immensely full and high is
Their love for all in the world.
O, when the wind is wafting over you,
Your voice is carried round the listening globe, o my sequoia!

IX

Indestructible giant sequoia!
Visible token of goodness,
Compassion, and care for the world!
Deep in my heart I'm being moved today,
For I've been hearing your whisper of greatness, wisdom, and truth.

X

O *Sequoiadendron giganteum*,
Noblest and fondest of beings.
Your soul is loved in the world,
And in my life you'll always grow higher
while I'm hearing your soaring divinity uplifting us all.

THE TREE OF MY CHILDHOOD

Where is the tree of my
childhood, mangos dropping
overnight in the yard, and
steel blue skies peeking over
the fence the next morning?

Who told me back then to
open my eyes, and when I did,
why did sun-drenched tears
start running down my face
on seeing what was gone?

Come sunrise, find me on the
streets, squares and plains.
The vast expanse of space
between you and me should
not hinder our final union.

Come earth, cover my eyes,
my nose, ears and mouth,
now that I've seen such bright
sunlight on such simple things:
a house, a fence, a tree stump,

my hand holding a mango
that was not there . . .

THE LANGUAGE OF TREES

I

I asked the trees one summer
What they had been thinking of all year.
They wouldn't say,
But then I heard them wave
And whisper of the ages—
Seasons—
Years, and months, and days—
And countless hours
Of abundant happiness.

II

I like the tales they tell me.
Autumn makes them talk of leaving all,
And yet they stay,
And as they drop their leaves,
They muse for weeks on April—
Thrushes—
Stars and lingering Indian summers—
Rain—
And latent loneliness . . .

III

Their voice is low in winter.
Snow and icy winds are on their minds,
And they withdraw;
But in their winter dreams
You hear how branches sing,
And think of dawn—
The sun in distant countries—

Warmth—
And summer peacefulness.

IV

How grand they are each season!
Often have I seen them stand like kings!
A certain awe
Surrounds their splendid forms,
And so they wait for spring—
For flowers—
Verdant prairies—
Butterflies in May—
And simple loveliness.

V

And then they speak of lovers.
Sudden colors spread their message fast,
And every year
Their many stories bloom,
And brighten noble pages—
Poems—
Gorgeous music—
Heart and mind
With endless youthfulness.

VI

And so we welcome summer . . .
All day long they stand, and think and dream,
And all we hear
Is how they wave again
And whisper of the ages—
Seasons—
Years, and months, and days—
And countless hours
Of unending happiness . . .

LEAFLESS TREE

My roots went deep
To the center of time.

From the center of time,
A tree has grown.

My leaves were green
In the hands of the past.

Thru hands of the past,
A storm has blown.

My leaves came down
In the garden at dawn.

In the garden at dawn
The wind died down.

A leafless tree
In the silence of this.

In the silence of this:
My leafless crown.

WHITE BLOSSOMS

In shimmering rays from above,
white blossoms deeply in love
with drowsy spring
are humming, "spring, spring!"

Where those blossoms abound,
bright colors all around
awakening now,
are whispering, "how, how?"

White blossoms in their prime,
now in full flowering time,
all basking in love,
keep nodding, "love, love!"

DISTANT MOUNTAINS

and the shadow of mountains
will not fall on your heart.
—Sara Teasdale

Clouds on certain days resemble distant mountains.
I'm watching such a mountain now, and far below
Could be the perfect, crystal lake of dream.

On days like these when lakes reflect a silver heaven,
The air will shimmer mirrored like on shining glass,
And over distant clouds the sun will cross the lake.

But when the light is bound to sink behind the mountains,
Glimmering through the clouds as if there was the moon,
The night appears and slowly gathers round your quiet face.

On nights like these, your eyes turn monochrome and inward,
And when you close them, darkness covers earth and sky,
And yet I've seen the perfect dawn you dare to dream,

For on a certain night you turned to me to find my eyes,
And when you did, I saw a bright and crystal day
With mountains in a lake, and every cloud was gone.

THE HOLY MOUNTAIN

Among the many holy sites in India, there is probably none as sacred as a certain mythic mountain. It sits in a remote, almost inaccessible region where the entire atmosphere, animal and plant life, and even the soil are completely permeated with divinity. A pilgrimage to this mountain is regarded as a significant step towards spiritual liberation.

A devotee relates:

I traveled to the Region
Where the Holy Mountain Reigns.
I found such Simple Blessings
There, and lo, they Eased my Pains.

The Lofty Cedars waving
In the Dusk loomed Grand and Wise.
They've seen the Age—Old Craving
And Surrender God inspires.

I climbed the Towering Slopes of
Loneliness, and there it Was:
The Haunting, Inner Call of
Quiet and its Hallowed Cause.

The Shadows, stilled in Wonder,
Slowly darkened by the Brake.
A Deer was gazing Yonder,
Steeped in Love as was the Snake.

They Would Not harm each Other,
Neither did they seem to care—
A Human from the Valley
Also Headed for the Stars.

I felt the mounting Ecstasy the
Soul instills when Truth arrives.
The Time had Come, and Every
Tread atoned for Many Lives.

The Silence was a Silence
Springing from a Sense of God,
And from the Sky a Wondrous
Grace descended to This Sod.

The Ground could not be Softer
Where I Walked in Deep Esteem.
A Dove on High Extolled a
Path I Saw once in a Dream.

A Trail went Winding to the
Top into the Peaceful Night,
And There I Hailed the Vista
Of the Holy Land of Light.

WAITING NEAR THE THRONE

The night—the long, secret night—now covers all.
There exists a somber hour that isn't
Quite of this world. It dwells
Behind the dim appearances of forms we
Thought we knew. How dark they are,
Immersed inside the stillness — the Immeasurable...

Dawn is at hand...
Dawn... All of nature knows and waits...
And all at once every bird awakes to hail the dawn:
Dawn! Sublime window to Infinity!
Dawn! Dawn!! Glorious, visible Throne
Of the Eternal! *Dawn! Dawn!! Dawn!!!*

THE BOND

Green was the pasture,
but searing the heat;
so sluggish my doggie,
I slackened her lead.

She sniffed the still air
below and around her—
then ran from me there.
*Some*thing was stronger.

How far did she venture
if panting for game?
I'm circling the pasture,
still calling her name.

A Bright Side

In the valley of gathering shadows,
I walk a bright and worthy trail.
It's my joy to roam vast meadows,
And live this life and tell the tale:

It's leading to an open space
Of warm and most alluring rest.
I feel the sun across my face
May like to tarry high... far west,

Because the arc of life right now
Aligns with light that doesn't fade.
Look, the valley is all adlow,
Embracing a blond, delightful shade;

But even had I rather walked away
To weather storms and years of rain,
I'd meet my shadow side another day,
And maybe no one ever lives in vain.

Thus my shadow, like my darker side,
Is truly like a dear, old friend
As we're keeping to a brighter side,
And walk as one, clear till the end.

A SUMMER DREAM

If you can spend a perfectly useless
afternoon in a perfectly useless
manner, you have learned how to live.
—Lin Yutang

Summer sometimes means to me:
Strolling down the avenues
Of bright and rediscovered happiness,
Or—on a sultry afternoon—
Musing in a sunny park
And see the world go by.
Nothing else is on my mind today—
A love for summer colors must
Have drawn me to this ample lawn
To view the wide diversity of green
From where I'm freely watching now
The calm and overwhelming sky.

Everywhere around the spot
I'm resting on, I see how grass
Is bowing down and springing back again.
The density of heat and air
Evaporates and falls away
Like bubbles floating down a stream.
Gazing through the countless apertures
Of foliage overhead, I sense the
Pressure of the hidden years is gone.
I feel reborn, and this I know:
Whatever happened to me then,
Today is real and not a dream.

Down the rolling slope, a pond
Lies shimmering like a fine gem.
The heart of summer now reflects in it.
How good it is to see the sun
Envelop all my life again
And join the seasons through the years.
Warmth I hadn't quite explored before
Is slowly making sense to me

179

With all the joy of many summers past,
And suddenly I realize
How true my feelings have become,
Outlasting many long-held tears.

What I'm finding out is more
Than anything I could have known
Before I stepped outside to meet the sun.
A warm idea has touched my face,
And something tells me that my life
And perfect happiness unite.
Close at hand upon a rise, a grove
Sits smiling in a midday dream.
A tranquil light pervades the scene indeed—
A light it is where sorrows fade
And shadows shorten by each tree
When noon ascends and all is bright.

High above me in the sky,
Some tiny, birdlike forms appear,
And as I'm watching them, they soar unheard
Across their blue domain. I share
With them a hymn of thankfulness,
And surely God can hear their play.
Nature truly beckons everywhere,
And every single bird comes out
From tree and shrub and grove and lawn,
And all the hillside peals with song,
And while I reap the deep reward
Of reverie, I praise the day.

Myriads of crickets seem
To be around this year to chirr
Continuously with ecstasies, sublime.
Their thrilling choruses create
A ring of trembling harmony
Around the sunny days that pass.
Never was such music more profound—
I've closed my eyes, and timelessness
Descends like light upon a waiting soul.
I am alone and not alone,

Surrounded by my boundless self
To leave me breathless on the grass.

Children playing in the park
And parents calling from afar
Do not disturb my dream. The sounds
I hear combine with rising memories
Of long gone days and deep blue skies
When I—a kid—would catch a ball . . .
Sunken, long-forgotten images
Come rushing to my inner eye—
The loveliness, the charm, the innocence
Become as tangible as then.
It is as if I really hear—
And yet he's gone—my father call . . .

Idle thoughts in solitude
With simple pleasures last a day,
And then they sink with flowers past their
Prime. A lesson dwells in each of them,
Regardless of their brevity,
And yes, they live to fade away.
Leaning leisurely against a tree,
I live to see these truths, and now
The season's bloom is drawing to a close.
Eternal summers are fulfilled.
I am content and I embrace
The perfect splendor of today.

Echoes of a carefree time
Are fading in an avenue
Of verdant quietness across the lawn.
I've touched the grass, the pond, the air, the sun
Since summer has become my home,
And so I have discovered more—
Summer sometimes means to me, thank God:
Dreaming away my time like now;
And yet I've simply felt in tune with all. It's
Getting late—I'm heading home.
The sun is going down—I trust
That happiness sits blazing by my door.